mourning sickness

Stories
and
Poems
about
Miscarriage,
Stillbirth,
and
Infant Loss

Edited by Missy Martin and Jesse Loren

Published by OmniArts, LLC.
P.O. Box 51612, Phoenix, AZ 85076-1612
For more information about this book and its contributors visit
http://mourningsicknessbook.blogspot.com

Cover artwork "Stillbirth on Black Paper" by Marcia Milner-Brage

omniartsllc.com

Library of Congress Control Number: 2008921724
ISBN 13: 978-0-9788489-1-0
Printed in the USA
First edition, May 2008

Acknowledgements:
"Black-Eyed Birth" by Steve Montgomery was previously published in a slightly different form in *Black Rock & Sage*, 2006; "Childproof" by Susan G. Duncan was previously published in *Iodine Poetry Journal,* Fall/Winter 2006/2007; "Counterpoint" by Carol Barrett was previously published in *Poetry Northwest* and the author's collection, *Calling in the Bones* (Ashland Poetry Press, 2005); "Falling to My Knees" by Shelli Graff Angel was previously published on *Literarymama.com*; "Long After the Loss" by Maureen Tolman Flannery was previously published in *JAMA Journal of the American Medical Association,* November 10, 2004; "Miscarriage" by Elizabeth Schott was previously published in *Zone 3*, Spring 2007; "Still Moment of Mystery" (c) Kathleen Willis Morton, 2008, is reprinted from *The Blue Poppy and the Mustard Seed: A Mother's Story of Loss and Hope*, with permission from Wisdom Publications, 199 Elm Street, Somerville, MA. wisdompubs.org; "Waiting" by Lisa Lenzo was previously published in *Within the Lighted City* by The University of Iowa Press, 1997; "Writing Around the Word" by Julie Danho was previously published in *West Branch*, Fall/Winter 2005, Number 57.

Contents

As if to contradict me, a contraction begins, the same huge hand stretching and probing now, pressing too hard. The hand feels vicious, as if it wants to hurt me and also to test me, to see how much stirring up, how much messing with I can take. It makes me think of the hand of a torturer, and I wonder how such a feeling of evil can be part of the beginning of life. I think of the child I dreamed, and now that pink light washing over his skin makes me think of water tinted with blood. I think of that pink, bloody light covering my child and make myself stop. I decided at the beginning of this pregnancy that I wouldn't cry anymore, and for the past nine months I've managed to keep myself steady. Just wait, I remind myself now, looking around at the brown basement walls, the pipes running along them up near the ceiling. It's so quiet down here, buried beneath the earth, as if the surgeons chose this place to help them with cutting downward and inward.

ANOTHER PAIR of green-clothed women appear on either side of my cart. The taller one touches my strapped right hand, checking the IV tube; the other one lifts my free left arm, holding it up for the taller one to see. "Oh, that should have been restrained," the taller woman says.

I want to pull my arm away, but there's nowhere to hide it. The short woman starts to tie a strap around my wrist. "Don't," I say. "My doctor said I could have it free."

"We're tying it loosely, see?" the tall blond woman answers.

"I can't have it tied at all," I say. "I'm going to use it to hold the baby after he's born."

The short woman hesitates; she doesn't knot the cloth.

"You're not going to hold your baby anyway," the tall woman says, not realizing the threat in her words. Again I feel the shark swim up, the water turning nightmare black. "Caesarean babies are taken immediately to the nursery," the tall woman explains. "And if your arm isn't restrained during the operation, you might

contaminate the sterile field. You don't want to contaminate the sterile field, do you?"

"I'm not going to," I say. "I'm—"

"Well then it has to be tied."

The tall woman and I continue to argue, in level voices. The woman keeps asking me if I want to contaminate the sterile field; I keep telling her that I'm going to keep my arm out of the way of the operation and that I have my doctor's permission to have my arm free.

We've drawn an audience of green-clothed people; six or seven of them stand in a loose half-circle around my cart. I know that my arm will have to be untied before the operation so the anesthetist can inject the spinal, but I'm afraid that once I'm tied down, though they'll free me for a moment, they'll tie me right up again afterward. With the last birth, that's how it went, in rapid steps— no, in leaps—from a natural birth, to a standard Caesarean, to being knocked out without my permission or even my knowledge, to never seeing my baby at all.

Finally the tall woman says, "Well, you can talk it over with your doctor when you see him. For now that arm is going to have to be tied." The short woman knots the strap, and the green-clothed onlookers look disappointed. Everyone walks away. I lift my arm like a dog testing its leash. There are three inches of strap between my wrist and the bed rail. My other arm, taped to the IV board and strapped to the other rail, is completely immobile, as are my legs, belly, and feet, bound by the deeply tucked sheets. The hand inside me tightens into a fist, then spreads its fingers and digs, and digs deeper. Again I feel the shark. He's so close I can't tell where he is.

I'M WHEELED to the operating room, where a fat, fair-skinned nurse and a dark, wiry anesthetist are waiting for me. The nurse untucks the sheets and methodically unties the arm that the other

women and I just made such a fuss over. Then the nurse and the anesthetist help me onto my side. "Do your best to get into a fetal position," the nurse says.

I curl around my big belly and close my eyes tight, and the anesthetist walks his fingers down my spine, feeling for a good place to insert the needle. A cold wet spot appears on my back, and I smell alcohol. "So," the anesthetist says in a chatty voice, "how many children do you have at home?"

I feel as if I've been struck. I lose my breath. Then my body convulses, and I can't hold back my sobs.

I can sense the nurse and the anesthetist beyond the wall of my crying, beyond my heaving body; they're waiting for me to stop, or to explain myself, or for a clue about what they can do. I know that they must have a good idea of why I'm crying, but suddenly I need to tell them; I can hardly speak, but I want to pull the truth out of the dark. The words come out of me in pieces: "My—one—baby—died."

I DON'T realize that I've been gone until I come back, to the sound of my crying, and the weight of two soft hands pressing my shoulder and my hip, and two leaner, harder hands resting against my back and the back of my neck. It feels as if they're holding me together.

The nurse suggests I try breathing deeply and slowly, and I try it and it works. It's as if I'm learning to breathe for the first time; all I hear and feel is my own breath as it leaves and enters my body. "Okay," I say. "I'm ready now."

Again I curl in on myself as far as I'm able. The anesthetist fingers my spine, and the cool wet spot reappears. "Hold perfectly still now," he says. There's a pause, an absolute stillness.

I don't feel the needle going in, but the anesthetist says, "Finished," and he and the nurse help me onto my back. The nurse re-ties the arm strap quickly, unthinkingly, as if she were re-tying

a shoe. Then she goes to the door and lets in a group of green-clothed people, among them Ray and Dr. Cal.

As soon as all of them have taken their places, I raise my left arm the few inches that the strap allows. "Can I have this arm free?" I ask, looking into Dr. Cal's eyes, the only part of him not hidden by cloth.

Dr. Cal looks over my head, and I can tell that his friendly, piercing gaze is looking right into the anesthetist. "What do you say, Doctor?" Dr. Cal says. "You're never going to get a better patient."

This might be a lie. I don't know how I'll react. Dr. Cal wasn't at the last birth. The doctor who was knocked me out seconds afterward, before I could suspect that something was wrong.

The anesthetist must nod or shrug his agreement. Dr. Cal picks up my wrist, and, with a scalpel that has appeared in his hand like magic, he slices the strap in two with one stroke. I take Ray's hand in mine and face the cloth screen rising above me and the table. Now things will move fast. Now the waiting is as close as it can be to being over.

A SCALPEL stings across me like a fingernail tracing a line; then the whole inside of my belly is moving as if the baby is wrestling with the doctor's hands. It doesn't hurt, but it's frightening; it feels too powerful, more than my body can bear. Then a sudden, tremendous absence exists, as if someone has knocked me hollow.

"It's a girl," someone says; *a girl* I think, and before I can ask to see her, she is being held above me. Her skin is a bright, deep blue, the way the sky gets sometimes in fall, on the clearest, most brilliant of days. I can see right away that she's healthy and strong. Ray sees it, too; he says into my ear, "She looks good, Annie, she looks really good."

The baby is twisting and struggling in the doctor's hands, crying and fighting the bulb syringe suctioning liquid from her mouth.

The bulb syringe follows her struggling head, and she twists the other way, breaking free.

Beneath the baby's crying, I notice a strange sound, coming from somewhere close. It's a sound like I've never heard, human and inhuman, stranger than the blueness of my daughter's skin. I listen to it with no idea of what it is until I realize it's coming from me: a low, keening moan; sad, hopeless, inconsolable; but what makes it so strange is that it isn't sustained—it starts and it stops, broken by my laughter.

My baby stops crying and is placed in my arm. She's breathing deeply and beginning to turn pink; pink is overtaking the blue, starting from the center of her chest and spreading outward, washing over her like water, like light.

A Memory or Its Ghost
Douglas W. Milliken

angela and I drive up to Mum's farm, through the pineland belly of Maine to its eastern border with New Brunswick, to plant a tree. Her olive-tan Italian hand rests on my lap, in my earth-red Scottish hand as the wind whips our hair, whips our voices out the windows onto the highway, out among trees and rivers and mountains and birds. It's a beautiful blue July day, the sort where the transparency of the sky reflects the transparency of the earth, but mid-way a blinding thunderstorm falls upon us like a lion or a god, manifesting insanely—ferociously—then disappearing, leaving us again in a see-through, unlikely landscape.

What can you do when nature so vengefully turns against you, then just as immediately takes it all back? We stop somewhere for dinner, stop again later on for an ice cream cone. So it's dark when we finally roll in. A milky splash of stars. The slow breathing of a land peopled with no people: rustling leaves and heat-singing crickets, foxes dashing through tall grass. We wait until morning to plant the tree.

SYRINGA RETICULATA. From the Greek and Latin, literally a network of pipes. Out on the lawn, the Japanese tree lilac we brought for Mum stands tall and symmetrical, grey bark like a cherry tree, its matrix of upward branches forming a chalice rich and green.

"Wow," Mum breathes, blinking in the morning sun, sleepy-dazed and happy to have me home. Her softly aged hand reaches

to touch my much harder hand. "It's like a big lollipop."

We decide it will go by the greenhouse. To guard the southeast corner of the farm as a shading leafy beacon. To bloom with flowers like white captured clouds. While Angela watches and waits, I explain to Mum how the tree will grow, its habit and patterns, what she can expect it to do. Explain as if to a child the mechanics of an elaborate toy. Explain as if this was not a trick but a gift.

DANIEL DIED died before I was born, before he himself could be born. Her obstetrician wasn't at the hospital when Mum went into labor, and not knowing what else to do, the nurses held Mum's knees together until the doctor could arrive. By the time he showed up, the contractions had clenched to a suffocating halt. Danny's ashes have been in a little blue box under the bed-frame in my mother's bedroom ever since. Waiting as these years.

I do not believe in ghosts or spirits, but I do not disbelieve in them either. It's like the many shapes and colors of religion: for people who believe in ghosts, there are ghosts. Perhaps tied to places or events or epochs, like a monument at a battlefield or an icon in a church. Or maybe when I say ghosts, I mean a sort memory. Something essential and tangible, imprinted on a place or in a person. The echo of an empty room. A hand cradling an empty belly. So I guess Mum has kept a box of unrealized memories hidden in the dust and dark of her bedroom. I guess I've decided to set those memories free.

I DON'T mention anything until the hole is already dug. I do not want Mum to have time to think about things, to make things elaborate or ritualized. Whenever the topic has come up in past conversations, she's described impossible scenarios that she's now too old to accomplish: climbing a mountain, hiking far out along some coastal bluff. Her creaking hips and smoker's lungs, her sixty years and innumerable trials, all add up to an improbability, yet its

her idealized dreams that make it impossible. I don't want to give her a chance to make this moment impossible. So I don't mention anything until the hole is already dug.

My stepfather has borrowed a backhoe from a farmer down the road, and within a few minutes he has a good-sized trench dug, nicely shaped but far, far too deep. Two feet wide, two feet down, maybe four feet long.

Do I recognize these proportions to be so figuratively close to a child's grave? I do not. I see only a hole that is too big for the tree I intend to plant. Yet I also see the hole as where my brother will soon be interred, his unfulfilled memory resting forever. So maybe, indirectly, I do understand this dark gash to be a grave. Angela and I half-fill the hole with compost dug from the pile beside Mum's garden and set the tree's root-ball into the moist, black earth. Mum stands by, watching, and is actually about to leave—to head into town to get some groceries, to leave us be since we clearly have the situation under control—when I ask her to go get Danny.

"Get who?" Then: "Oh." An eastward breeze blows a stray length of grey hair from behind her ear to cross her eyes. Mum goes inside to get my brother.

THERE ARE far fewer ashes than I remember there being. When I was a little boy, no more than four years old, Mum would some-times have me sit beside her on her bed. She'd open Danny's box and take out his bag of ashes, let me sift my fingers through my brother. His ash would stain my fingers, bits of bone rolling in-side my palms. My memory of those instances made his box—his plastic bag of ashes—seem so much fuller, much greater, but no: just a couple handfuls. Mum and I empty the ashes into the hole, she gently tossing, me working the dust in among the roots. Then she and Angela and I pour more compost over the tree's roots and tamp it down, get out the hose and make sure my brother has had

introduction

Losing a baby is a crushing event whether it happens at the start of pregnancy, or further along as hormones and hope are coursing through the body. The reactions of family, neighbors, friends, and co-workers may exacerbate the grief. Often the loss leads to feelings of isolation for those who suffer it.

Mourning Sickness is a collection of poetry, memoirs, and fiction rooted in each writer's personal experience with miscarriage, stillbirth, or infant loss. In their own words and style, mothers, fathers, grandparents, children, and others bravely share their journeys through this difficult terrain.

Reading *Mourning Sickness* is like curling up on the sofa and hearing your closest confidant's most personal stories. The content is at times filled with wisdom and wonder, and at other times filled with fear and denial. Some of the stories include cultural and religious influences. Together, the stories normalize grief, and create inter-connectedness among those who have endured it.

There is much to glean about life, loss, chance, and moving on in this collection that is really about hope and the indomitable spirit.

breathe
in

Falling To My Knees
Shelli Graff Angel

a plate of scrambled eggs with sun-dried tomatoes, feta, and spinach sits before me, but I cannot eat. My saliva tastes metallic. People at neighboring tables share stories over coffee. It's like any Saturday morning at the Tea House, and we look like a regular family enjoying brunch together.

Nothing is regular about this morning. Cramps rack my body. Perspiration jumps from my pores. I ask Rick to get the car. I need to go home. Now. Please. He leaves and I ask for the check. Sara draws a Crayola masterpiece on the napkin, oblivious to the panic simmering within. "Let's go sweetie," I pry from my lips. My eyes betray me; faces lose clarity as if I'm trapped in a blender. I stand and pick up my daughter's coat, and lose consciousness.

HEARING THE news that I'm pregnant again is like having cotton candy for the first time. Rick walks through the kitchen door with balloons for me, his very nauseated wife. "Let's call everyone!"

"Shouldn't we wait? It's so early."

"I'm excited! I want to call everybody."

I sit down, holding my stomach. "I don't feel very good."

"That's so exciting!" Rick blurts. He kisses me, then floats to the back door, and prances outside, shouting, "Love you!"

I smile, inhaling his joy, and think how handsome my husband looks with his goatee and salt-and-pepper hair. I drag myself out of the chair and make my way down the hall to our bedroom.

How ridiculous, the term "morning sickness" is. For me, it's "all-day-and-night sickness" coupled with sheer exhaustion. All I want to do is curl up and go to sleep. I sink into my bed like an anchor thrown overboard. Another baby. A sibling for Sara.

SITTING ON the lime green couch reading *Parent* magazine, I wait for my first exam since learning of the pregnancy. My unwelcome friend, nausea, is finally gone and I feel like myself again.

"Shelli Angel?" the nurse calls.

I follow her into the exam room, undress, and put the two-by-two sheet over my lap. It is always so damn cold in these rooms. I look at the ultrasound machine next to me. I'm at ten weeks now, and I can't wait to see the first picture of my baby, and hear that beautiful strong heartbeat.

Doctor Ruby Weiner, 35-ish, blond and blue-eyed, struts into the room. I am reminded of one of my favorite Barbie dolls.

"Hi Shelli."

"Hello."

"So, let's see. You're about ten weeks." Dr. Weiner smiles a business-like smile, then takes out the Doppler heart monitor. "Let's take a look."

The tips of her narrow fingers are cold as she rubs gel on my stomach. She places the monitor on my lower abdomen and searches, moving in slow concentric circles. She lifts the monitor and tries another area.

"Is something wrong?"

"Not necessarily." She makes no eye contact, just focuses on the Doppler monitor and my belly. Finally, she gives up and offers that cordial smile again. "I'm going to do an internal ultrasound."

I put my feet in the stirrups. I watch the blonde girl turn on the ultrasound machine, and I enter a surreal, comic strip world where everything is flat and two-dimensional. The room is a vibrant shade of pink; Doctor Barbie is a doll—plastic, all boobs and hair. She speaks in cheerful little smiles and rhymes:

"Well, I see the gestational sac,
but it's empty… whoa is me.
This may feel like quite a smack,
you'll need to have a D and C."

Journal Entry 10/30/01

I feel like I was just hit by a truck. I've been imagining, planning, and dreaming about this baby. Now it's gone. Three
months of my life—two spent so whacked out, nauseated,
and tired that I couldn't function; and one recovering from
the D & C procedure and the aftermath of "here today, gone
tomorrow." Maybe I should get checked. I'm nearly 41 and
not getting any younger. Sara is almost three. Shit. I had Sara
at thirty-eight. Why can men keep having children until they
are 80?

WHEREVER I go, I see pregnant women. At the grocery store,
at the coffee shop, at the gym, at Sara's preschool. They are everywhere. Following me. Tormenting me. It's a conspiracy. I must be
the only woman in all of Boulder, all of Colorado for that matter,
who is not pregnant.

"I was fine three years ago. Why is it different now?" I ask the
fertility doctor.

"You never know," Doctor Schooner tells me. "After 40, fertility drops significantly."

"So, it will be harder to get pregnant?"

"Look, you failed the Clomid challenge test. Your eggs are inef-
ficient. If you get pregnant, which is doubtful, you will miscarry,"
Dr. Schooner says like a CEO reporting on my company's finan-
cials.

"Why?" I ask, holding back tears.

"As you age, your eggs age. Your egg quality is no longer good."

"Don't I have any good eggs? Not even one?"

"No. Not even one."

ROTTEN EGGS. I have rotten eggs. I walk down 13th Street, pass the Boulderado Hotel, and turn the corner toward the Book Cafe. I wonder if people are looking at me, aware that I have rotten eggs.

I argue with Schooner in my head. There's always a way. I'll simply make it happen. I'll be like I was when I was 15—a figure skater training for the Olympics. So, I have bad eggs. It's a terrible fall, but it's time to get up, dust off the ice, and try again. I know about effort. I'm good at self discipline. I can do this.

It's the height of spring in Boulder; thousands of multi-colored tulips line the Pearl Street Mall in a magnificent palette of every imaginable shade of pink, yellow, orange, and red. I breathe in the crisp air and feel the warm Rocky Mountain sun shining down on me. A pregnant woman walks by. They're everywhere. Crossing Broadway, I think of my friend who had in-vitro fertilization four times and finally decided to use donor eggs. Then, there's the woman down the street who tried to have a baby for 12 years before she and her husband decided to remain "child-free." I'm now part of that club, one of the millions of women battling infertility; another woman who desperately wants to have a baby. Maybe it's a longed-for first child; maybe a second or third. For one reason or another, all of us have been deceived by our bodies, betrayed by our empty wombs.

I drag my heavy body, weighed down by its own failing, toward the gate. I open it and walk into the playground. Sara runs out of her classroom with her red curls blowing in the wind. Her smile lights up her peaches-and-cream skin, and her deep brown eyes fill her face from ear to ear.

"Mama!" she cries as she runs and jumps up, wrapping her legs around me. I hold my three-year-old daughter. I never want to let her go.

Journal Entry 12/31/01

2001. One big miscarriage of a year. I'm so grateful for what I have in my life. To be alive. But, I still want more. Two children, my dream. Is that greedy? I started Chinese acupuncture yesterday. Tang told me I'm "depleted" and that if we work on my "chi" energy and on my kidney and liver energy (whatever that means) we can increase the vitality of my eggs. Okay. I'll do it. I'll give myself six months to clean up my system. I'll take the herbs, cut out coffee and sugar, and eat red meat. Hell, I'd eat a side of rare beef in one sitting if it would help. I will prove Doctor Schooner wrong. I will make it happen. I'm not the kind of person who fails.

As I prepare for my double axel, a shiver runs through my body. For this moment, I'm alone in the center of the ice. Round and round I go. I fall and lift myself up, ready to try again. There's no such thing as failure. I can do it. I will do it. Rounding the corner, I begin my preparation. I turn and jump into the air, only to fall once more. Again and again. Spinning, turning, flying, jumping. I am at home in the cold, dank, grayness. Determined, I build up speed, step forward onto my left leg with my arms and right leg back, spring up into the air, pull my arms and legs in and—spinning like a top—I land with precision, that thin metal blade balanced perfectly on the ice.

SITTING ON the exam table, I flip through a magazine, not paying attention to the words on the page. It's been a year since the miscarriage. The blood tests show that, so far, this pregnancy is good. Rick sits in the chair next to me, tapping his foot on the floor. After what seems like eternity, the doctor walks in.

"This little flicker is the heartbeat," Doctor Madison says. "Everything looks just perfect."

I see it—a tiny light—flashing on the screen.

The doctor takes out her wheel. "With a heartbeat, there's only a five percent chance of miscarriage. When was your last period?"

"December 15th."

I look over at Doctor Madison, a woman bordering 50, whose warm, compassionate eyes and long gray hair look at home next to her long flowery skirt and Birkenstocks. She turns the wheel to find the magic date.

"You're due date is September 21st."

Tears tumble out of Rick's eyes. Sitting next to me, he embraces me, and breathes easily again. "I was really scared."

"We did it," I whisper to him.

"No love, you did it. You said you'd do it and you did."

Doctor Madison leads us out into the lobby. "I'll see you two in a couple of weeks. Congratulations."

Outside, Rick looks at me with that look he had when we got married, when his cheekbones were permanently raised. He kisses me goodbye and jumps on his bike. I open the door to my white Ford Explorer, climb into the driver's seat, close the door, and put my hand on my belly, feeling the life inside of me.

THREE WEEKS later, Sara stands in the backyard with the baby-sitter as Rick and I get into the car. "Bye mama. Bye daddy." I wave to Sara as Rick pulls out of the driveway. I am silent as we head toward the highway. Finally, I can't hold it in any longer.

"Sara says I don't have a baby in my tummy."

"What?"

"She's been talking about having a baby brother or sister, and I told her you never know what might happen."

"And?"

"And, she said, well, you don't have a baby in your tummy now, Mama."

Rick puts his reassuring hand on my leg. Then, with a flash of hesitation says, "Oh honey, I'm sure everything is fine."

EVERY TIME I close my eyes, I see the ultrasound picture. The fetus, hopelessly floating, heartbeat silenced. Why did this happen again? I did everything right. I didn't drink coffee. I took my vitamins and herbs. It's been two weeks since my second miscarriage and I can't stop crying.

I sit in the playroom on the floor with Sara. She hands me her baby doll.

"Pretend Baby Hannah is my baby sister and you're our mommy," she says.

"Oh honey. No. Why don't you do it," I answer trying to save myself from the still-raw pain searing through me.

"No mama. You hold her." Sara places Baby Hannah in my arms across my chest. "You nurse her."

I look up and see myself in the mirror. My face twists and my heart wrenches as I dam the river of tears. There I sit, next to my four-year-old child, rocking Sara's baby sister in my arms.

Journal Entry 3/20/03

People don't ask how I am doing anymore. They don't send food. They don't send cards. After all, it was "just a miscarriage." "It wasn't meant to be," they say. "Better now, than later." "You can try again." I simply go through the motions. Even with Sara, even with how much I love her, I am lonely. I mourn for the potential, for the life that came and left. Rick just goes through the motions too. We both know the routine. After a while, we won't mention it anymore.

I WAKE up on the cold floor in the Tea House, surrounded by strangers looking down at me. I am flat on my back. Sara is lying over me. "Mama!"

"I'm okay honey," I tell her.

Am I okay? I think.

"You fainted," Rick says, as the paramedic checks me. Cramps roar inside me. Miscarriage number three. The man takes my pulse and puts an oxygen mask over my mouth. I am going to vomit. I hear them say my pulse is 30, blood pressure 70 over 40. *That's not good, is it?*

I try to stay calm, taking long, slow breaths. I watch the double doors of the ambulance close. I think of Rick and sweet Sara; she doesn't understand what is happening to me.

The man pokes my arms, over and over again. Then, my feet. *What is he doing?*

"I can't get a vein," he says after what feels like an unbearably long time. "I'm going into the carotid artery."

"I'm gonna be okay, right?" I ask through the oxygen mask.

"That's what I'm working on," he replies stoically as he connects the IV to the stint in my neck.

I tell him, "I'm cold."

It's colder in the rink than usual. My breath dances from my lips as I pad my ankles with foam and lace my skates. First my left. Then my right. It's quiet with only three other skaters carving figure eights into the crystal ice. I take my place on the ice and stand with my arms out, finding my bearings. Like a mathematician, I measure my block of ice. Like an artist, I prepare my canvas before sketching with my steel blades. Like a Buddhist monk, I calm my body and center my mind. At fifteen, I am a girl who has found my calling and nothing will stop me. I will not be defeated. I will not fail.

I LIE in the hospital bed. Rick sits by my side, holding my hand. My blood pressure and heart rate are stable. I, however, will never be the same.

Eventually, I will get up, dust myself off, and walk on, living the life I've been given. At forty-two, I am a woman who has surrendered to the fact that she is not always in control. I have learned to lose sometimes, to let go.

Sara walks into my hospital room and stands next to her father. "Mama!" she cries. "Mama okay?"

"Mama's just perfect, my angel." I look into the faces of my husband and child. I know the balance this takes—the cold edge of metal on ice, the precarious takeoff, the difficult landing, and the delicate, hard-earned dance that follows.

The Miscarriage
Katherine Cottle

The fetus' shadow enlarges
across the screen,
one small lump
surrounded by
pulled strings of tissue.
I already know the answer,
have known since
the blood started,
since I began waking up nights
with an empty pit echoing
in my stomach.
There should be a heartbeat by now
and I know the technician is trying to warn me,
to send the early flag down
before she passes the Kleenex
and lets me get re-dressed.
I take one last look
at the shadow,
at the knot that could be
any random part of my body:
the pulled tendon of a finger,
a small cross section of the brain,
any part that doesn't move,
that never wakes up.

fetal demise
donnarkevic

friday

my old man waits
outside in his pickup anxious
to get back on the road he worries
about speed traps the price of diesel
about having another mouth to feed
says it's my fault not being careful

the doctor doesn't look at me
tries to explain the test results
I stop listening after he tells me
I detect no heartbeat
there's nothing
I can do you'll have to wait
until after the weekend

I start feeling like maybe it is my fault

when I get back to the vehicle I tell
my husband he's quiet drives as I cry
later he paces half an hour around the living
room then vanishes on a four-day run

saturday

I prepare meals I do not eat
as I lay on the couch my live child rests

her head on my belly she grieves the baby
sister I promised I tell her god wanted her
for company his house so full
of empty rooms but by jesus
I don't believe god cares
to have another child again
let alone worry about mine

after I put her to bed
I dismantle the crib

sunday

I fold maternity clothes box them
maybe I'll mail them to my sister-
in-law expecting twins this spring

I visit the grave of my mother who died
birthing me my father remarried for love
alone could not raise a child he feared
just as I did when my first husband left
me with a two-year-old

monday

after the school bus disappears
I sign in mock-maternal a cut-
out mother to a paper child

my canopic womb bleeds
the wound gives birth to silence
I ask to see her someone cradles
a doll baby in my arms the weight
nothing more than the universe

Childproof
Susan G. Duncan

To open, push down and turn
We embrace with
urgent design, fixing
ardor in tenths of
fahrenheit, forcing
passion into fortnight
program, and pretend
it's as easy as
falling into bed.

Close tightly
We clutch at
hopeless expectancy,
willing against the routine
hemorrhage, the quiet
carnage like clockwork,
the slow
bloody leak
in the hapless vessel.

Keep out of the reach of children
No tiny hands risk
mishap here,
much less
our holding.
No tiny Dutch boy's
tiny fingers
ever come
and seal the rupture.

Waiting
Lisa Lenzo

i shift my weight on the high hospital bed, take a quick, deep breath, and let it out like steam. Ray looks up. "How are you do-ing?" he asks. He's sitting across the room on a blue plastic chair, a tan lunch tray abandoned on his knees.

"I'm doing fine," I say, meeting Ray's gaze, trying to gauge how he's feeling. But it's as if he's a lover I haven't yet learned to read. "Come check out your kid," I say. "He's moving just a little— stretching, I think." Ray sets aside the lunch tray and walks over to the bed. During my first pregnancy, Ray would rest his hands on my belly, he would press his cheek close, and also his lips. But now Ray only touches my belly with his fingers, and his touch is light, and his smile is like a ghost's.

Ray returns to his chair, and I look at the VCR screen, at a tape on breastfeeding that a nurse has put in. Filling the screen is a softly smiling mother and her nursing, contented child; the baby is alert, gazing into its mother's eyes.

Dr. Cal reappears in the doorway and says, "Annie? Ray? We can have an operating room at two-thirty. How would you like to meet your baby half an hour from now?" Ray and I nod and smile. All three of us are grinning as if we're about to open some big gift; inside me, where the gift lies, a contraction begins. It feels as if a giant hand is spreading there, thrusting outward through all my flesh, the huge fingers pressing too hard, threatening to hurt me badly, but holding back for now. The threat of worse to come makes me think of the last time I gave birth, and it's as if a shark

14

has risen into sunny water, swimming up from lightless depths. Dr. Cal and Ray don't seem aware of the threat right now. Maybe they're just pretending to be oblivious of it. I keep smiling, pretending to be oblivious, too. But I remind myself not to get too happy, that there's power here far beyond our control.

DR. CAL leaves the room, taking Ray with him, and two green-clothed women walk in and get to work. They help me into a gown, insert an IV needle into my right hand, tape that hand and arm to an IV board, and strap the board to the bed. "You ladies move fast," I say, trying to get them to look at me. "I feel like I'm at a car wash." The women smile but don't meet my eyes; they're too busy. They shift their hands to the base of my big belly and wash and then shave the top of my pubic hair, where the incision will be made. The scar from last time is still noticeable. The knife will enter at the same place.

But this will not be like the last time, I'm almost sure, although we are at greater risk.

Ray and I haven't talked much about it. It's as if we're on separate boats heading for the same shore. I'm holding my boat steady, Ray's holding his. It's all that we can do for now, almost more than we can do. Later we'll meet up again, when this is all over. Meanwhile our boats surround us like empty shells. Dr. Cal flutters above our bows like a bird and flies ahead toward where the shore will be, if it is there.

THE TWO green-clothed women drape a sheet over my outstretched legs and big belly and tuck it tightly all around so I can't move. But I tell them to leave my left arm free—I want it to hold the baby—and they do as I say, they leave my arm unrestrained and outside the sheet. Last time both of my arms were tied down, and they took the baby away without letting me see her. This time everything will be different, I tell myself again, and I think of the child I dreamed.

He was sitting on my kitchen counter with red sunlight washing over him. The light rippled like water, its redness turning him pink. He was sitting up by himself. He looked healthy and strong. I woke up feeling someone had made me a promise. My promise dream, I call it in my head, my true dream, even though I don't always believe in it.

When I told the dream to Ray, lying beside him in bed, Ray didn't say anything. I could feel him holding himself somewhere far off. We've lived together for five years, since we were 21 and 18, but it's felt to me this past year as if we've been living apart.

Last fall, two months after the birth, we took a trip to Isle Royale, a gift from my parents intended to give us solace and time alone together to help us regroup. My parents arranged for lodging and meals for a week, but Ray and I left at the end of the third day. To me, each day on the island felt seamed in by sadness, a pouch of sadness that enclosed all the land, lake, and sky, but I felt better there than I did at home. Still, nothing I said could convince Ray to stay. As soon as we reached the island, my menstrual cycle resumed, and Ray was afraid I might be pregnant again and miscarrying. I tried to assure Ray that I was all right, but Ray didn't trust my judgement or our luck. He felt panicky, he said. Even if I weren't miscarrying, so many other things could go wrong, with me or with him. Anything could happen, and the nearest hospital was half an hour away by plane. I pointed out that we had been far more isolated four years ago while backpacking in British Columbia, but Ray only said, "Yes, I know that. I didn't realize the risk we were taking."

THE GREEN-CLOTHED women finish their prep work, and an orderly wheels me to the elevator and takes me down to the basement, leaving me by myself in a windowless hall. All I have to do now is wait. I've already waited nine months, plus the nine months of my other pregnancy, and the three months between; a few more minutes will be easy, I think.

Perhaps they are not stars in the sky,
but rather, openings in heaven,
where the eyes of our loved ones behold us
and shine upon our journey.

an Eskimo Legend

For Corinna

a good drink.

But there's also this: As we filled in the hole, Mum found a snake. It was in with the compost I'd shoveled out from the garden, that I had wheelbarrowed to the tree and dumped into the hole. He was tiny and grey-black like old coals from a barbecue. Mum held him for a moment in the earth clumped to her hands. Then he slithered away into the grass and was gone, and we finished burying my brother.

I had expected there to be tears, but there are none. Even in my idealized, minimalist fantasy, I had expected catharsis and purging. Yet it's such a simple thing, and then it's done. And now my mother's son is a tree.

Now my brother is a tree.

Shipwrecked
Marcia Milner-Brage

*I*t was Halloween. It had been raining for days, a hurricane-driven, whipping downpour. The James River had flooded the tobacco warehouses in downtown Richmond. A sodden sweetness of steeping tobacco wafted uptown to our house. I had spent the afternoon making Jules' costume: a blue corduroy cape with red satin lining, a fake-fur beard with an elastic strap, and an aluminum-foil-covered Masonite saber. He was three, and this was his first time trick-or-treating. With his candy bag bulging, pirate Jules splashed gleefully through puddles in the blustery darkness. I slogged, big-bellied, behind. As we rushed to get back inside, uneasiness snagged me: *the baby hadn't moved. The baby had been utterly still. No kicks. No flutters. No hiccups. No elbows to my ribs. No knees to my bladder. Had it been for the whole day?*

Later that night, I lay on the daybed in the study. Our nurse-midwife, Nancy, leaned over me. A stethoscope connected her ears to my eight-month mountainous belly. Nothing. No sound of life.

FOR A week I was pregnant with a dead baby. Jules and I stayed home indoors as it continued to rain. We played trains, made little boats glued together from scraps of wood, and read and reread the latest stack of library picture books. I grappled with the unthinkable: *the baby would never move again.* As Nancy had instructed, I drank increasing doses of blue and black cohosh tea to encourage my body to push the baby out.

At last, my uterus took up a lazy rhythm. At last, the sky was

26

cloudless and calm. The silver maple in the front yard had turned completely gold, but had not yet dropped a leaf. My parents came from out-of-town to care for Jules at a hotel. Mirabai, another midwife who was experienced in complicated home births, came from Yogaville—Swami Satchidananda's ashram in the Blue Ridge Mountains—to assist. She arrived just as my water smacked the bathroom floor.

I lay on a low futon in my art studio, a room that was to become the new baby's bedroom. I had painted it the color of tomato soup, the color of the womb. Sunlight sneaking through the closed Roman shades made the room glow like a fleshy hull. Nancy and Mirabai swathed my back and belly with flannel compresses soaked in a warm ginger brew. John held me and murmured encouragement. All of us breathed in unison. And then the baby slid out: silent and blue. He was broader and hairier than his brother. His eyes were dark and sunken beneath transparent eyelids that were fused shut. His mouth was flaccid—it knew no sucking. His fingers were curled and stiff, their tips wrinkled and boggy. He and I lay side-by-side, shipwrecked, the cord still connecting us by the un-birthed placenta.

Later, I wiped him dry and swaddled him, as if he were alive. We named him Ivan. I opened the shades and watched the leaves drift down from the maple outside, and we shared a holy silence.

Black-Eyed Birth
Steve Montgomery

We are at Shakey's eating chicken and pizza and MoJo potatoes. I am thinking that MoJo potatoes are about the closest I've come to food paradise. Perfect little ovals of flavor, crispy and seasoned on the outside, chewy on the inside. I always love it when we come to Shakey's on all-you-can-eat night. I have one entire red plastic basket piled high with MoJo potatoes, and another one filled with chicken breasts and sausage pizza.

Just above a tired pinball machine with a broken left flipper hangs a torn projector screen, and Dad and I are laughing as the Three Stooges take turns knocking each other silly. Mom's not laughing. She's never liked the Three Stooges. Normally, she would be telling us how un-funny she thinks they are, and why, but tonight she's pretty quiet.

When Mom gets up to go to the bathroom, I get up to refill my orange soda. As I'm filling up my glass, one of the cooks says "Shit!" and I watch him fly from behind the counter to the projector. I spin around just in time to see Curly being consumed by a giant black spot. The cook manages to stop the projector before anything catches on fire, and Dad literally applauds his efforts, embarrassing me in the process. Next month, I will officially be entering junior high, so I have enough to worry about without my father bringing even more unwanted attention my way.

Soon, the film is replaced, and the Stooges are once again cavorting about on screen. I ask Dad why Mom is taking so long in the bathroom. He seems unconcerned. Until another five minutes pass.

He gets up to see if anything is wrong. Even over Mo's obnoxious patter, I can hear my father's voice.

"Dani? Everything okay?"

A few minutes later, Dad returns to the table. It's clear that something is wrong.

"Your mom's having some female problems and we have to go get them checked out."

Mom emerges from the back of the restaurant. She looks pale and she's holding her purse at an odd angle in front of her. Dad immediately puts his arm around her and helps her to the car. My job is opening doors.

I find out in the car that Mom used the purse to hide bloodstains that continue to spread across the lap of her white polyester pants. The only thing of any use that Dad could find in the trunk is Mom's bowling towel, which she is now using to blot the blood. In typical Mom fashion, she is concerned about getting blood on the front seat of the Impala.

WE ARRIVE at St. Anthony, hospital of my birth, and Dad helps Mom into the emergency room. A nurse tells us she will be right back with a wheelchair, and I stay with Mom while Dad parks the car.

"I'm sorry, honey. I really ruined your dinner, didn't I?"

My face goes red with embarrassment. It is exactly the kind of thing my mother always says at moments like this. In my head I scream at her: *Dinner?! You think I'm worried about DINNER at a time like this?* But even at eleven, I've learned that this is my mother's way of asking for reassurance. And that is what I do best at moments like this.

"Mom, of course not! I'm just worried about you. Are you okay?"

She smiles and tells me that everything is going to be fine. Dad returns from the parking lot and the nurse returns and wheels Mom away.

Dad is filling out paperwork, and I am watching as others watch me. A woman is cradling her coughing infant, shaking her head at me as if to say, *You poor thing...you poor, poor thing.*

THE THING is, my mother is seven months pregnant after eleven years of trying. Soon after I was born, the doctors told Mom that she would never conceive again. My birth had been a particularly complicated one. I had managed to position myself in some awkward way that made it difficult for the doctor to deliver me. So he used forceps, and there was nothing gentle about his methods. He gave me quite a shiner around my right eye. The story of my black-eyed birth has been told and retold to family members so often that I can repeat it as if I remember it first hand.

I got off easy. The bruises went away. But I had damaged my mother. I remember Mom telling me it had something to do with her fallopian tubes, but I knew it had everything to do with me and my unruly entrance into the world. So this pregnancy was a surprise—a welcome surprise. Welcomed by my parents, and welcomed by me. Finally, some relief from the guilt I'd felt all these years.

Dad comes over to tell me that he is going to "find out what's going on." He points to a pile of magazines on the table next to me, then digs in his pocket for some change. His face is weary, like he just got home from one of his graveyard shifts.

"You'll be okay here. Here's some money." And then he walks down the hall.

Just when is about to disappear around the corner, he turns his head back and glances at me. He is wearing the same expression as the woman with the coughing infant.

I pick up a *Highlights* magazine and try to find objects cleverly hidden in the wild overgrowth of some exotic jungle. By design, everything is out of place. A hammer hidden among the leaves of a plant, a slice of pie barely visible in the mane of a lion, a sailboat stranded in a treetop. *A boy in an emergency room waiting for his mother to reappear.*

WHEN MOM told me she was pregnant, I was excited and relieved. There is good news and bad news about being an only child. The good news is that there is no competition for your parents' attention—you get it all. The bad news is that there is no competition for your parents' attention—you get it all. By age eleven, I was beginning to feel smothered by all that attention, especially my mother's. It felt like I alone was responsible for realizing all of her hopes and dreams. And since it was my birth that had prevented other births, I felt a powerful sense of obligation to be whatever my mother needed me to be. It would be a relief to have someone around who could bear some of that burden.

But now there's a problem: *Unanticipated bleeding. Female problems serious enough to need checking out.*

A NURSE comes over to see how I'm doing. She tells me her name is Wendy and offers to buy me a Coke, but I tell her that my dad has given me money. She walks me to the vending machine. We turn the corner where my mother and father disappeared, and for some reason I expect to see them both coming down the hall, but only nurses and orderlies and doctors pass by. I buy a bottle of Coke and a Snickers bar.

Nurse Wendy is asking me questions like how old I am, and whether I have any brothers and sisters. As she deposits me back on the waiting room couch, she assures me that everything will be "just fine." She brings me a blanket and tells me that if I get tired it's okay to lie down on the couch.

Long after I finish my Snickers and Coke, I begin to wonder why Dad hasn't come out to check on me. It's after nine, and although I'm not tired, I try lying down to see if sleep can silence the confusion in my head. The coughing baby is gone, and the only noise comes from the nurses behind the counter, laughing at stories I cannot hear, and answering telephones that seldom ring.

"STEVE?"

My father's voice awakens me. He has been crying. I am still in the fog of sleep interrupted as he struggles to tell me the news.

"Your mother has given birth. The baby was stillborn. It was a boy."

These are the words I hear. There are others, but these are the ones that emerge from the fog.

My father is on his knees. He begins to cry again and I realize that I have never seen my father cry. It frightens me more than the news he has just delivered. He buries his head in my blanket and I do not know what to do.

Soon there is a Lutheran pastor doing the things that I cannot. He pulls my father aside and consoles him, and then returns to console me. He tells me that I may not understand it now, but that all of this is in God's Plan. *This was planned? Doesn't that make it worse?*

I bear his false claims and coffee breath with the hope that he will soon leave me alone. He's talking as if a living, breathing human being had died. Our neighbor, Mrs. Manning, had a miscarriage last year. One day Mrs. Manning was pregnant, the next time we saw her she was not. That was it.

Isn't this the same thing?

"These things happen," I heard her tell my mother. "We'll just have to try again."

Isn't that what Mom will do now—just try again?

The pastor leans in so close I can feel his white beard brush against my ear. "They named your brother Jeffrey. It means 'Bringer of Peace.' Isn't that a beautiful name, Steve?"

This catches me completely off guard. They named it? I don't understand any of this. Maybe this pastor, a man I've never seen at our church, is just making this up. Maybe he thinks it will make me feel better to have some name to hold on to. He's wrong. It just confuses me. *My brother?* I had seen no wrinkled red face, no heavy-lidded eyes. Whatever I had not held in my hands, whatever had not puffed baby breath against my cheek was never truly a brother. *Was it?*

I begin to cry and I don't stop until long after Dad tucks me into bed.

Still Moment of Mystery
Kathleen Willis Morton

i was changing my son Liam's diaper when I noticed his left hand and part of his arm had started to turn dusky-plum blue.

"Liam," tears came again, "you have to let go now, baby." My knees sank to the floor. I folded over the bed where he was lying and pulled him to my side. He was so thin it hurt me to hold him.

"Liam, if you need to go, you should go." I had been repeating that phrase for forty-five days when I could gather the strength. Every day, I knew it might be his last. I gave him permission to die. Hospice workers and Tibetan Buddhist tradition say to do that so the person can have a peaceful death. I was desperate to give back something to Liam, even if it was only a peaceful death. Every night as I held Liam bundled up between his father and me in bed I thought, *Please not tonight. Just let him live until the morning.*

Every morning I didn't move until I knew that he was still breathing. Then I'd kiss him, and I'd think, *not today. I hope he doesn't die today.*

When I saw his hand was blue I knew it wouldn't be long.

"You can't hold on any longer, Liam. It's time for you to let go."

My father-in-law, who is a heart surgeon, had told Chris, my husband, and me that Liam's limbs might discolor eventually because his heart didn't circulate enough blood.

My voice was soft and shaky like a butterfly flying against the

34

wind when I finally got Chris on the phone at work.

"Chris, you have to come home. His hand is blue. You have to come home."

"I'll be right there."

Chris had only been at work for a few hours, and it was only his second day back. He didn't want to go back to work, but we had no idea how long Liam would live—and we had to reach for some normalcy, now almost seven weeks after his birth. When we left the Neonatal Intensive Care Unit at Emmanuel Legacy Hospital, Liam's cardiologist had said, "If he's still here in a week, call me. I'll want to see him again."

When Liam had been home a week we decided not to call the doctors anymore.

"Will they be able to tell you anything that will make a difference in his condition?" my father-in-law had asked.

"No," we'd answered, remembering the grim diagnosis that was documented in his medical records:

> The child has sustained extensive bilateral cerebral hypoxia. This seems to be a more global change that would suggest more of a global perfusion problem, rather than emboli . . . The prognosis, which is very limited for this child, has been discussed with his family. His prognosis is of such severity, I think the family should be apprised of this in order to make decisions on his care.
>
> I would support their decision either way, to avoid futile care (in view of his very serious neurological findings) . . .

Futile care. That was the phrase that hit me the hardest. How could it make sense that medical care for any child would be futile?

I FINISHED changing Liam's diaper and swaddled him in a blanket. I put a hat on his head even though it was June 27th. He should have been fat and warm, bouncing and giggling on my knee. Instead, I took his temperature every couple of hours to make sure it had not slipped below ninety-two degrees. If it were really low, Chris would unbutton his shirt and undress Liam to his diapers. Then they would lay, bare chest to bare chest, under the comforter, with the light streaming in the bedroom window, until Liam was warm again.

Liam's eyes were dulled and glassy. He was somewhere trapped inside a body that, at the time of his birth, had looked perfect in every way on the outside. His skin was downy like a white peach. He had our coloring. His hair was amber, a subtle blending of his father's auburn-brown and my strawberry blonde. When he was born a plump 7 pounds and 8 ounces, he resembled me. Then his cherub frame waned to probably less than 4 pounds. I had books on my shelf that were heavier than he was in the end, when he took on the sharp angles of his father's face. Inside—his heart and his mind, his wisdom, and his skill—he had reached his fullest potential at almost seven weeks old.

"He won't walk. He won't talk. He won't be able to feed himself. You will be lucky if he recognizes you as his parents." Liam's neurologist, had said at our initial meeting. With each sentence he spoke, the tide of my blood pulled back. I felt my face blanch, and my jaw and body slacken. "He might not even be aware of his surroundings. And I'm not sure he'll even be able to think. Let me make this really clear. I'm not talking about mild damage. I'm not talking about medium damage. This is severe." His eyes were unwavering.

CHRIS ARRIVED home. But that was all we could do—just be with him. I didn't want to put Liam down. I sat in the white chair by the bookshelf and held him. I picked up a thin copy of *The Life of the Buddha* by the Venerable Dr. Hammalawa Saddhatissa, and

I began reading it out loud to Liam. I sat, and read, and held my son all day because I couldn't bear to let him go. I didn't know anything else to do. I didn't want to do anything else. I didn't get up to eat or pee. I sat and held my son all day. Chris was across the room sitting on the couch for most of the day too. I didn't fully notice what he was doing. I just felt the barely-there weight of my son in my arms as I read to him about an ordinary person who had found a way, a path, out of suffering.

That night, I lay next to Liam on the bed. I turned on the TV that was at the end of the bed. I didn't really want to watch TV. I just didn't want to watch my son die. The square room felt like a TV screen. I watched from outside myself. I saw Liam on the bed wrapped in his blankets: motionless, silent, still breathing. I sat next to him, propped up on the pillows, and stared at the happy everything-will-be-okay-in-a-half-hour world on TV. I was still on the surface like a calm ocean, but underneath I was dark and shifting restlessly. I felt I should be talking to Liam. I felt I should be doing something. I felt I should hold him and comfort him. I flicked off the TV and turned to him. Each breath could be his last. I didn't want to miss it, but it was too hard to focus my attention on him. I tried to talk to him.

"Liam, Mommy's here. Don't be afraid." Hysteria rose to the surface of my voice like a shark with obsidian eyes. I gasped and choked on my words. I couldn't talk to him and stay calm at the same time. I didn't want to disturb his dying. I didn't want to distract him with my moans and cries that might hold him to this imperfect body and world. I turned the TV back on and watched

every crisis resolve on the half-hour. I floated above my grief. Chris was upstairs meditating. My son lay dying beside me. Though I couldn't look at him, I felt the rise and fall of his breath throughout that Thursday evening, and into the night when all three of us curled up under the covers and let the dark of the room enclose us.

That night I didn't make my panicked plea for one more night. I just pulled Liam close and whispered with my lips touching his soft cool temple. "Mommy has you, Mommy has you." I wasn't sure he could hear me, but I hoped that he could feel my words.

The moment of Liam's death came gently near dawn as he lay on the bed between his father and me.

I heard a little whine just as I was beginning to doze off. I was instantly wide-awake. "Chris, turn on the light." I looked at the clock; it was 1:58 AM. Liam whined again softly. He took a breath, and then did not. I moved the blankets away from his body so I could see it. Chris and I were vigilant for I don't know how long. Liam was lying on his right side with his right arm bent and his palm beneath his head. His left arm was folded across his chest with his other palm down on the bed. By chance it was the same position the Buddha was in when he passed into *parinirvana*. Chris and I were propped up on our forearms lying on our stomachs beside him. Liam's belly and chest did not rise again. We were still. The world was still. It was the moment we knew would come. That mysterious moment that connects this life with the next. The only moment that all of us can be sure will eventually come someday.

We rose slowly and sat on either side of the bed. Every bit of warmth left his body as I sat reciting, as best I could, the Tibetan Buddhist prayers prescribed for the moment of death. I closed my eyes. I heard my cries as if from a distance. I forced myself not to cry so that Liam could pass away undisturbed. We didn't touch him. I didn't want to hold Liam back. In that mysterious moment, this is what I remember seeing in my mind: There was amber light. There was warmth. There was a person with long hair and a beige dress with her back to me who squatted down, opened her arms, and scooped up a plump, pink, laughing baby who kicked and waved his arms. I thought the baby must be Liam though I didn't completely recognize him in a healthy body. The woman walked away, carrying the baby who was looking over her shoulder. I felt calm. I noticed I had stopped choking on my dammed-up tears and gasping for breath. As I slowly opened my eyes I heard a small voice say, "Mommy." With my eyes then fully open, a thought popped into my head. It was Liam, and he knew I would want to hear him speak just once. It hadn't occurred to me until just then that I would never hear my son call me *Mommy*. And yes, I would have wanted to hear it. Those were things—speaking, laughing, thriving—that he would never do, no matter how long he lived.

I turned to Chris and looked over his shoulder to the clock. It was 5:30 AM. Three and a half hours had passed into nothing.

"We should clean him up before he gets too stiff," I said. "Will you do it? I can't."

Chris had to do a lot of things I was not strong enough to do.

PRETENDING everything was okay was something I could do, had to do sometimes, and was something I got good at faking for short amounts of time.

When Liam was four weeks old we had to buy him preemie clothes because all his newborn clothes, hand-me-downs from my sisters-in-law and crisp new outfits from his baby shower, were all too big. We went to the same store where we had ordered Liam's blue-and-white gingham stroller with a chrome chassis and white-wall tires. The saleswoman recognized us. We had spent a long time with her while placing our order for the stroller and had spoken to her several times on the phone. As we looked through the small selection of clothes for premature babies she was silent. She didn't congratulate us. She didn't come over to dote on Liam. I could feel her sad eyes on us. She looked away when I looked up to meet her gaze. I tried to pick the cutest onesie from the sad assortment on the rack for my son who was not born prematurely—just dying that way.

Chris and I loved to push Liam in his buggy up and down Hawthorne Street by our home and pretend we were a normal family.

"Oh, he's perfect," the man at the Ben & Jerry's shop said. He put his arm around the pregnant woman standing next to him and gave her a gentle squeeze. What we couldn't see behind my perfect son's soft, dark eyes was the tremendous global brain damage that robbed my son of the most basic of human survival instincts: to nurse, to cry, and to respond to the world around him.

"Yes," I said to the man. "He's perfect."

We encountered another couple on the street. "Oh, a redhead. We have a redhead too," said a woman holding their two-year-old.

"Just wait till he's this age," the man gushed to us. "They're such a blast."

"We can't wait," we beamed back.

Some people did notice that there was something a little different about Liam. "What a cutie," the owner of the bar on the corner said screwing up her nose. "He's got some snot on his cheek, though."

"No, that's his feeding tube. He's very sick."

"Oh." She didn't skip a beat. "Isn't it amazing what they can do with science these days?"

"Yeah," we both said. We just smiled. We didn't tell her that it was more amazing that science could do nothing for us, or for Liam.

"So, have you adjusted to the shock of being new parents yet?" she asked.

Chris and I stared at each other looking for an answer.

"I guess that means no," she said.

We were in shock but not because we were "new" parents. Parenting a terminally ill newborn, assessing all the information the doctors delivered to us, and deciding what was best for Liam, we felt like we had done a lifetime of parenting in just a week. We had never had time to feel new.

CHRIS DID, however, take care of Liam with the adoring attention that any new father would, till the very end.

Chris went into the bathroom and ran hot water over a washcloth to clean Liam for the last time. He returned and pulled Liam, who was still lying on the bed, a little nearer to him so he could change his diaper. Chris turned Liam on his back. I winced and turned my head away. The right side of Liam's face and the corner of his right eye were dark cherry-red with still blood that had begun to pool on the side of his body on which he was lying. His eyes were basalt, skin like lilies-of-the-valley, lips the color of gray-blue flannel.

As I stood up I saw Chris cleaning Liam's bottom, wiping away the tar-like excrement released when his energy let go of his body. Chris held Liam's cold feet and wiped him clean with slow, deliberate strokes, taking care to make sure he wiped away all the dirt, just like he did every day in the same gentle manner. He did not grimace. If he was too overwhelmed, like I was, to touch his son's cold, dead body, he didn't show it.

"I'm sorry you have to do that honey," I said, "I just can't."

"It's okay. He's my baby. I love him, and I want to clean him." His voice was a thin trickle.

"I'll call Sharon," I said leaving them alone in the room. Sharon was Liam's hospice nurse who came over every other day. She didn't sound as if I'd woken her when she answered the phone, though it was dawn.

"Sharon, it's Katie." My voice was flat.

She said, slowly raising her voice to make the one word into a question, "Hi?"

"Liam passed."

Sharon exhaled. "Okay. Do you want me to come over now or

do you want some time alone with Liam?" She knew some people were afraid to be alone with their dead children. We had talked about what would happen when the time came. She had to come over to officially pronounce Liam *dead*.

"No, you don't have to come now. He actually passed away at 1:58, but we didn't want to call you then."

"Okay, I'll come over in a couple of hours. Did you call the funeral home?"

"Not yet."

"Do you need me to call for you?"

"No."

"Okay, I'll see you in a couple of hours."

Chris called the funeral home. The man who answered told Chris that they wouldn't be open till 9 am. We were grateful to have a few extra hours with Liam. We lay on the bed with Liam between us.

"Maybe we should read him *Horton Hears a Who!* one last time," I suggested.

Chris's voice undulated with tears held back as he read. It was the story we read to Liam every day when he was hooked up to all the monitors and IVs for the first week of his life that he spent in the NICU, the Neonatal Intensive Care Unit. Chris dissolved into tears half way through the story when he read, "I'll just have to save him. Because, after all, a person's a person, no matter how small."

We reached over Liam to each other, and cried, and waited.

The Consequences of Moving
Patricia Bell Palmer

*b*eth was having a miscarriage. That's what the doctor told her when she called to inquire about the pain and bleeding that had started that morning.

What kind of bleeding was it, the doctor wanted to know. At first, a quarter-sized dot of thin, bright blood, Beth explained. She could not help noticing that it resembled a cheerful, chubby valentine in the middle of the crotch in her panties. Sexy, except for its implications. She did not tell this to the doctor. She did say that the blood continued to flow, and that it now resembled the gluey, blue-black ooze of a period.

A period. Beth tried to mask her panic, but she felt her lip curl when she said it. The irony of the word's dual meaning had grown painful for Beth and Owen over the past three years as they tried for a child. Both English teachers, they enjoyed the flirtatious banter of word play. But when Owen sheepishly revealed that each month had become for him a 30-day sentence ending in a period, Beth had felt a chill. Sex, once miraculous in its intensity and spontaneity, had become a scheduled exercise, a chore. Still, they joked to cut the tension.

"It's like mowing the lawn," Owen told her.

"Climb on," Beth said. "But don't expect a response. I feel like I've been spayed."

When months of the same material turned into a full year, their jokes subsided. Then nine weeks ago, a store-bought pregnancy test changed their lives. Owen waited outside the bathroom pestering her and making her laugh while Beth saturated an absorbent wand with urine. She laid it flat on the sink and opened the door, gesturing elaborately.

"Come and witness my masterpiece. I call it, 'Piss on a Stick!'" They hovered over it, full of longing and skepticism. Owen had a hard time staying serious. He waved an open palm over the sink.

"Eenie-Meanie, Chili-Beanie, the spirits are about to speak!"

"Shut up and watch, Bullwinkle," Beth said.

They both saw it at the same time. Barely visible. Undeniable. A second line. Beth grabbed the instructions and read aloud. One line: not pregnant. Two lines: pregnant.

"Do it over," Owen said. So they had. And again the next day. This month, for once, their sentence had not ended in a period.

UNTIL TODAY, although Beth had to remind herself that this was not a period. The pains were worse and more rhythmic, like waves at a cold, colorless beach. Every few minutes a fleeting stillness was interrupted by a rising sensation, a drawing in of the muscles deep and low in her abdomen. She wondered if this was what labor felt like, and again bit the soft, lavender stripe of her pillowcase, leaving a pattern of damp teethmarks along its worn edge.

As she lay perspiring, Beth's intellect taunted a purer part of herself, offering that while a miscarriage is not the same as a period, it certainly qualified as an exclamation point.

She relived her conversation with the doctor. Her hand had trembled when she dialed the phone. *Blood and pain. Were they normal?* Probably not, but she had not been prepared for the intensity of other symptoms her doctor had assured her were perfectly ordinary in the first trimester of pregnancy. She was surprised and relieved to learn that some cramping was normal. Unspeakable exhaustion that left her all but unconscious by day's end: normal. Bouts of vomiting during which Beth imagined her tongue as a fat, venomous snake, muscling down her throat, and spewing poison over the scrambled eggs, plain white toast, and ginger ale that were her only nourishment for six consecutive days: normal.

She lay on the bed drawing deep, measured breaths. The pain transported her to another dark time in her life, one she had not thought of consciously since she and Owen had gotten serious nearly three years ago. That other pregnancy. The one she ended by choice. The icy, ancient hands of a gentle doctor who seemed to whisper rather than speak. *Almost finished dear...it's almost finished...relax your legs...let your knees fall open...doing fine.* A yellow room with lights that felt hot enough to tan by and a smell that reminded Beth less of a hospital room than a musty coat closet. The warm and pulsing life within her growing. Growing. Gone. A bit like today but, strangely, not like it at all. She could handle the pain, but her thoughts were growing intolerable, so she pushed them away.

Then, as now, Beth would not take something for pain. She wanted to feel it. She was entitled to it.

It occurred to Beth that she also wanted to see it, but did not know what to look for, whether any part of what passed from her body would resemble a baby. Her baby. About to leave her. Period.

With the phone pressed between her ear and the pillow, Beth reached Owen in the teacher's lounge, grading papers. They rarely spoke during work hours. A colleague called him to the phone.

"Is this the mother of my child? To what do I owe the pleasure?" Owen's need to be constantly upbeat was sometimes embarrassing, irritating.

"I didn't go to work. I'm not well. And please don't make a joke."

He did not ask the questions she hoped he would. What was wrong? Did she feel a cold coming on? Headache? What exactly was the problem? Owen did not ask any of these things. Instead, he wanted to know whether she needed him right away because he had a mountain of freshman essays to grade and Grigoleit, that prick, had just asked him to sub seventh period and after that was the department meeting at 3:00 where he wanted his question about afternoon hall duty addressed once and for all....

"Just come home when it's over then," Beth told him. Owen said that he would. As soon as it was all over, he would come straight home.

She dropped the receiver into its cradle and sighed. Once again Owen had picked up on Beth's cues as easily as he might pick a dime off the floor wearing oven mitts. Beth had complained to her sister Lindsay, who was unsympathetic.

"Is it a man's fault," Lindsay asked, "that he's hard-wired for other things?" Beth had thought and thought about it.

She wondered how long the miscarriage might take. Could be hours. Beth had had a hard time believing her pregnancy was real. Now the fact that it was ending made it a striking truth.

SHE HAD expected a similar feeling back in 1985. When she got pregnant as a college sophomore in upstate New York, she and her then-boyfriend Leo opted for an abortion after a single night of sleeplessness and tears. Leo had wavered, but Beth had not, even when he cried out loud, saying he could not bear to kill any part of her. Leo, who saved an envelope in his sock drawer containing a thick, long curl he begged to snip from the back of Beth's neck one hungover Sunday morning. *Did he still have the envelope?* she wondered. Or was Leo, like Beth, left with only vague memories of their short-lived romance and their decision to erase perhaps the biggest thing they had ever done, together or alone?

Ultimately Leo agreed to drive her the following morning into Poughkeepsie to a doctor known for his sympathy toward reckless teenagers, for whom he believed the $175 bill for services was punishment enough.

The worst part of Beth's decision had been the anticipation of heartache, of guilt, of realizing too late that she had made a horrible mistake, of missing her baby. But none of these emotions had materialized. Because, she had decided with help from Lindsay, there had been no baby.

The pain from her abortion was only physical. After the procedure, she lay on her side for hours, imagining her uterus as a rag heavy with blood. Her uterus, or womb, was a muscle, the whispering doctor had explained, and its job now was to push pieces of remaining tissue—bits of fetus that the suction tube might have missed—out through her vagina. So Beth found it helpful to think of wringing a soaked towel into a narrow funnel, expelling more and more fluid with every twist. She lost consciousness twice from the pain, but refused the doctor's and Leo's coaxing to swallow a strong narcotic and sleep through the worst of it. "Take it yourself," she urged Leo, who looked ashen and weak.

The abortion had been a wise choice. At nineteen, having a baby would have done a terrible injustice to everyone involved, including the child. Lindsay assured her it was so, and Beth drank in her advice with relief and gratitude.

Afterward she drank four glasses of orange juice and felt mainly relief, marred by an ironic guilt that stemmed not from the abortion itself, but from her failure to feel ashamed in the first place.

Weeks later she ventured briefly into existential waters, but Lindsay again helped her regain sensibility.

"Stop asking who this baby was. It was nothing," her sister assured her. "Not a baby. Nothing. A batch of cells." She also said something that remained with Beth to this day. "It's only a baby if you want it. Understand, little sister? That's the difference."

So there had been no baby.

NOW BETH cried for the first time, trying to agree with what her sister had told her so long ago. Crumpled on her side, she found it comforting to draw on the memory of her abortion, even as she realized the stark differences between then and now. Then she had felt, perhaps falsely, unbearably alone. This time, she was not alone.

She struggled to summon the wringing sensation, hoping it would facilitate the inevitable, would ease her baby's distress more quickly. But the feeling would not come. It was not her choice this time. She found herself instead fighting the image of a sharpened tube slicing though a baby's spinal cord, or leg, or heart. Beth breathed deeply, determined to regain control of her thoughts. She was alarmed to hear her own voice, all but lost in the close dampness of the pillow. "This is different," she told her baby. "You're with me now." Her uterus undulated warmly with a distant but familiar burn of progress. She closed her eyes and pictured it, smoldering and hot, rhythmically coaxing a life barely begun from a state of distress to one of finality and peace.

Would she see her baby? Beth recalled facts from the volumes of literature provided by friends and family. She and Owen had shared the news after only four weeks. They made lunch dates with old friends to experience their reactions in person. Sent pictures of the sonogram to their parents, none of whom lived near their Brooklyn brownstone apartment. Composed corny, clever e-mails—poems and riddles—that prompted the most delightful, congratulatory responses.

Within a week, books started arriving at the apartment, complete with margin notes and tagged pages, most from friends who were already new parents. *What to Expect When You're Expecting, Your Baby and You,* and *The First Nine Months of Life.* She thought of facts from her most recent session with the literature. Twelve weeks. Her baby had eyelids, nails, and fingerprints. A skeletal structure, nerves, and circulation. Perfectly formed, tiny feet and toes.

Tiny feet and toes. Something to recognize. She wanted to see them. She dialed the doctor's office a second time. The doctor did not come to the phone.

"I have a question that I guess is a little strange," she told the nurse. No reply. "I am now fairly sure that I am having a miscarriage. But I'm wondering whether there's a way to know...I mean... to know when it actually takes place."

A pause. "Maybe. The cramping may suddenly become worse, and there might be pressure...Could you hold, please?" Beth lay at an angle, her torso stretched awkwardly so the phone cord could reach. It hurt. A lot. Thirty seconds. A minute. A minute and a half. A wave of pain brought her knees to her chest and she was aware of her voice as a raspy accompaniment to each breath she drew.

The line sprang alive again. "Hello, are you there? Anyway, yes, you can expect more cramping and maybe some pressure. Does that help you?"

Beth took a deep breath. "Well, I guess I want to know...will I see the baby? Will I recognize it?"

"That depends. The fetus may be expelled in a sac that could prevent you from seeing it, or it may be exposed. Don't worry. The fetus is very tiny, less than two inches long. Unless you look for it, you probably won't have to see it."

Fetus. Expelled. These words from the same nurse who last week had used words like *baby* and *birth*. Her shift in attitude and her assumption that Beth would choose not to see her baby, no matter how small, to greet it and touch it tenderly before saying good-bye, offended Beth. But unlike Lindsay, she had learned from her mother to stew silently at affronts like this rather than speak her mind, so she ended politely.

"Thank you for your time. Goodbye."

Was it the change in position that made the pain much worse? Or Beth's exasperation at the nurse and panicked realization, the certainty, that she wanted desperately to see the baby she was about to lose, but might not. Simply because he, or she, would be too tiny, too translucent and fragile, too unprepared, to pass in and out of this world without so much as the touch of Beth's fingertips. Her fingertips, she realized, would starve without that touch. She would starve.

Her uterus and the surrounding muscles of her abdomen, and now her spine and shoulders, roared and hammered like a tropical storm, vicious but strangely beautiful. Her baby would not go quietly. Beth closed her eyes, willed herself to relax. She repositioned herself and gently massaged her belly with one hand. She concentrated. And began to gain control. She inhaled through her nose to a slow count of ten, paused, then pursed her lips and exhaled to a five count. She imagined each breath as a gathering of pain and tension from all parts of her body to the center of her chest. As she blew out, she expelled them from her body. Her power was awesome. She closed her eyes.

Beth awoke with the startled revelation that nearly two hours had passed.

Was it over? The spasms had subsided. She stayed still in an effort to assess the progress. She remained curled facing the wall, the sheet still covering her to just below her waist. Her hands stayed sandwiched between her knees, her preferred sleep position since childhood, fused there by the moist warmth of flesh against flesh.

It was impossible to know anything without looking. But oh, the consequences of moving. She started to extend her legs beneath the sheet as a hot spasm shot through her lower back.

Beth realized she would have to give up her fetal position, would have to stand upright in order to drive the situation to its inevitable conclusion.

She sat up, then stood. Gravity took her body by surprise. She had been aware of a low, seeping sensation into the bulky, adhesive pad she had changed hours before. But now came a flood of warmth. A lot of blood, she knew, along with an undeniable sensation of mounting pressure. She steadied herself against the painted footboard, the pale yellow room a sudden swirl of deep blues and reds.

She had to get to the toilet, and made it across the bedroom in five long, crouched strides. Lightheaded and weak, she brought her panties to her knees and settled herself onto the chilly porcelain. She blinked into the overhead light, determined not to lose consciousness. In her peripheral vision, her underpants and pad lay limply between her ankles on the patterned tile floor. She couldn't look.

Her conviction wavered, perhaps a remnant from her experience with Leo nearly 15 years ago. She did not want to know or see. Not a baby. Nothing at all. It really is all a matter of how you think about it. She glanced between her knees and looked at her blood, thick and clean, not intended for its undignified place at the base of the toilet.

Never had Beth known such release or sorrow. The pad contained only blood, she was sure. It had not yet happened, but would at any moment. Was still inside her. More than cells. Her child. She could not let it slip from her body into the toilet— was not capable of forgiving herself, a mother, the inhumanity of such an act.

She pulled herself to a standing position and crossed the floor to the bathtub, recalling herself just days ago with bucket and brush, whistling on her hands and knees as the too-clean, gritty taste of Comet hung in the air. Pulling the curtain aside, Beth lifted one, then the other, bare leg into the tub. She engaged the drain stop with a dexterous, familiar flip of her toe.

The white tile was smooth and cool, yet the air was filled with soft, wet heat. She squatted.

Not five minutes later, she heard the click of Owen's key in the lock. How would he react to finding her this way?

She heard his voice at the far end of the apartment. "Beth? Babe? How're you feeling?"

Closer now. "Beth? Babe?"

Had his hand not been resting on the bathroom doorknob, had he not been pushing the door gently open at that moment, Owen would never have heard Beth's voice, tender and full of relief. It was a tone he hadn't heard her use before, and he would tell her weeks later that he briefly imagined her words were not intended for him.

"Hello. Hello. I'm so happy you're finally here."

A Moment of Life
Deborah Perkins

You sit cross-legged on the floor,
glazed eyes staring through the rusted screen door
at a Fourth of July sun blazing down
on the bare arms of browned farmers
baking in the fields.
Are you all right, I say,
just as you stand up and a dark circle of blood
gives testimony to where you have been.
Too soon.
The baby is coming too soon.
We all move at once—
Grandma screaming into the phone for an ambulance
that won't make it in time
and Mom laying you down
and me praying "Sweet Jesus, you've got to help me here."
But I guess even He takes a break now and then.

The child died in my own two hands.
Now she lies in a small graveyard
just off a dusty, gravel road.
Two uncles and an aunt keep her silent company there.
One lived a day, and one lasted a week,
and one survived just long enough to be missed.
Sometimes I put flowers on her grave,
a tiny doll, some baby toys.
The wind always bears them away.
But nothing disturbs her gentle slumber,
while I lie awake night after night

wondering what more I could have done.
Was it my fault?
Never to forget that moment of life,
wrapped forever around my heart
like lights on a Christmas tree
that shine so brightly for just a brief season,
before their glow is gone.

Discharged
Christine Simokaitis

We're at the playground when I first feel the cramps. I've just come home from work, and Tim and I have taken Caleb for his post-supper, pre-bath romp. After the short walk from our house to the park, I feel a stab deep in my abdomen and need to sit on the steps to the slide. Caleb has climbed to the top and is ready to come down. He pauses, making sure he has our attention before inching his body forward and sliding down. I say, "Weee," but my voice is flat. I'm worried about the pain that's marching across the left side of my pelvis. Tim looks over at me from the bottom of the slide where he catches Caleb and asks, "You okay?"

It was only this morning that I told him I'm pregnant, after confirming it myself with a home test. His expression now is less concerned than it is sweet. I want to think this is just the usual early-pregnancy discomfort so I say, "Just some cramping."

Once home, though, when I go to the bathroom and find a light pink stain on the toilet paper, I am scared. After Caleb is in bed for the night, I retreat to the basement to dig my copy of *What to Expect When You're Expecting* out of the storage bin where I had packed it away with my maternity clothes. It says that sometimes spotting or bleeding occurs early in pregnancy at around the time menstruation would normally take place. My period is only a few days past due, so I try to talk myself into believing that is what this is.

Back upstairs, I find Tim unloading several grocery bags filled with hot dog and hamburger buns onto our kitchen table. We're having a cookout tomorrow, a party Tim had volunteered to throw as a way of welcoming the new hire in the English Department where he works. All of his colleagues are invited. "Do you think we'll have enough?" he asks me as he attempts to make a pyramid out of the bags of buns.

"Sure," I say. We still have lots of cleaning and preparing to do for tomorrow, and normally I would start rounding up all of Caleb's toys from the hallway, kitchen, and dining room. Instead I say, "Something doesn't feel right. I think I'm going to turn in early." Tim looks worried now, and when he asks what's wrong, I tell him about the spotting. He winces and asks if we should call the doctor. I tell him what the book said, and that it's probably normal. I'm trying to reassure us both.

Early the next morning, though, after I've seen the dark red blood, there is little room left for consolation. I tell Tim, "I think I'm having a miscarriage." His face registers the grimness of my words. He hugs me and gently suggests that we call someone. I look up the number and dial the office of the OB who delivered Caleb eighteen months earlier. It's not yet 8 a.m. so the answering service takes my message. While I wait to have my call returned, Caleb shows me his plastic barnyard animals. I say "Moo" when he holds up the cow and "Baa" to the sheep, but mostly I'm just watching, distracted. I'm wondering what might have gone wrong.

It's not long before a nurse calls back. By this time the heavy bleeding from early morning has diminished, but I'm still alarmed whenever I go to the bathroom and find that I need a new pad. I never had any spotting during my last pregnancy. I tell the nurse I think I'm having a miscarriage. She says sometimes there is spotting, which is normal, but that I should be seen by someone, and get a blood test. She says I don't need an appointment, but since it's Saturday, the office will only be open until 1:00, so the earlier

I come, the better.

When I hang up, Tim says he thinks we should cancel the party. I'm feeling better now, though, having taken action, and I'm not ready for such drastic measures. I tell Tim to wait until I get back. "Everything might be fine," I say.

I've gotten dressed, had a few sips of the green tea Tim poured for me, and am gathering my purse and car keys when the phone rings. It's the doctor's office. They've now had a chance to pull my file and the nurse is informing me that they no longer accept my insurance. She asks me if I got the letter. It's hard to think. I do remember something from months ago. I had felt it didn't apply to me since at the time I wasn't in need of any gynecological care, and I'd been planning to switch practices anyway.

"What do I do now, then?" I ask. She says I really do need to be seen by someone and I'm still welcome to come to the office, but there will be blood work and maybe an ultrasound. She pauses to let the meaning of this sink without having to actually say, "It could be very expensive." She says that my primary care doctor might be able to get me an emergency referral to an OB, but since it's Saturday I might be better off just going to the ER.

Tim has been standing by, listening and looking worried, so I repeat this for his benefit: "The ER." Tim's eyes widen.

I hang up and call my primary care physician's office. I've never actually met the doctor who is listed as my primary care physician. I tell the man who answers the phone that I think I might be having a miscarriage. He asks me how far along I am. I tell him only a couple of weeks. He says I should be seen as soon as possible. He says I could come there, or I could go to the ER. He seems flustered. It's not clear what they're going to do, but he asks how quickly I could get there. I glance at the clock. It's just before 9:00. I tell him 20 minutes.

Now Tim wants to come with me. He is alarmed by the possibility of going to the ER and says maybe we should just go to the OB's office. I tell him what they said, about the tests, the ultrasound, that it could cost thousands of dollars. "Still," he says, "maybe it would be better."

I shake my head and tell him that the book said there isn't really anything that can stop a miscarriage. "I'm just going there for tests, I guess." As I say this, I realize I'm not at all sure what it is that I'm going to the doctor for. All I know is that they seemed to be pretty emphatic about me coming to the office.

Meanwhile, my cramps have resumed. I had felt a low rumble of pain while on the phone and now it feels like my uterus is clenching itself into a tight fist.

I call my parents to see if they could take Caleb. There is no answer. They live near the hospital where my doctor has her office. We pack some extra diapers, graham crackers, a book, and a plastic truck in the diaper bag, and I grab the key to my parents house on my way out the door.

I feel like we're rushing and moving in slow motion at the same time. At the doctor's office, there is checking in and waiting and telling the nurse I think I might be having a miscarriage because of the bleeding and cramping, and then there's more waiting in the exam room, all the while keeping Caleb occupied as he grows more tired and closer to needing a nap. When the resident comes in, Caleb and Tim have just returned from an exploratory walk down the hall and now the four of us, plus the stroller, are crammed into the tiny room.

The resident is young. He asks me what brings me in today and I tell him I think I'm having a miscarriage. As he asks me about how far along I am, and about the cramps and bleeding, he seems friendly and earnest, but nervous and uncertain about how to proceed. He is confused about my being here and not at my OB's office and when I explain about the insurance he is outraged on my behalf and launches into a long diatribe about HMOs and certain doctors. As he talks, I look past him to where Tim is standing next to the exam table, where Caleb is playing with the roll of crinkly paper that makes a wide stripe across the length of the table. Our eyes meet. We're both tense and annoyed. Caleb starts to cry; he wants another graham cracker. When the doctor says, "I mean, come on, how do you suddenly stop seeing patients just because..." Tim clears his throat and says, "So, now, what is it, exactly, that we're doing here?"

The doctor stops and looks at him.

"About the bleeding?" says Tim.

"Right," the doctor says and looks back at my chart. "Since it's only a couple of weeks, that means it's still your first trimester, right?" I think this must be a rhetorical question, but when he looks up from my chart into my face, it seems like he's actually asking me for confirmation. I'm now unnerved. He stands, clicks his pen and says, "I'm going to talk to my supervising doctor and someone will be right in to draw some blood."

He's out the door before either of us can ask any more questions. It's still not clear exactly why we're here, what it is anyone is going to do, or even if I am, in fact, having a miscarriage. I'm holding on to a sliver of hope that I'm not losing my baby as I sit here in this office, that the bleeding is just normal spotting and maybe if I rest and put my feet up, everything will be okay. I sigh loudly. Caleb is standing on the exam table playing with the little cone-shaped light that hangs on the wall, the one they use to look into eyes and ears.

By now I'm tired and hungry. I left the house in such a hurry, not thinking about any provisions for myself. I nibble one of Caleb's crackers, thinking maybe we should just go home. The resident comes back in. He is clearly more confident now. He has assurance, a plan. "Okay," he says. "We think you should go to the ER."

Tim drops me off at the entrance to the ER, then goes to park the car. Inside, I tell the woman at the desk that I think I'm having a miscarriage, and that the doctor was supposed to be calling over here to let them know I was coming. She scribbles something on a Post-It and tells me to have a seat.

I'm relieved to see that there are things for Caleb to play with here, big cubes in the middle of the floor with different activities displayed on each side, and bead labyrinths built into the wall about three feet from the ground. When Tim brings him in, Caleb goes right for the Tic Tac Toe blocks and spins them on their skewers. He's getting tired though, and I suggest that Tim take him to my parents' house and put him down for a nap. We both watch him for a while and when Caleb notices us looking, he runs over and buries his head in my lap. I pick him up for a big squeeze. "You've been sooooooo good," I whisper in his ear. He goes limp against my chest and tucks his hands under his belly the way he does when he's tired, they way he's done since he was an infant. I rub his back, feel his living, breathing body and am struck by an overwhelming wave of gratitude that he is here, with us, alive. He hums. I inhale his smell, squeezing my eyes shut against tears, trying to quiet thoughts of what might have been and of what I'm losing, right now, as we sit here waiting for my name to be called. Caleb jumps down and runs back to the wall, this time to trace the path of a red bead along a blue spiraled wire.

"Okay, yeah," says Tim. "Maybe we should go." He runs his hand through my hair. "I don't want to leave you though," he says.

Just then my name is called. "Oh," I say. "That was fast."

"Well, maybe we'll just stick around for a minute then, see what they say," says Tim, looking somewhat hopeful. But when I get to the desk, the receptionist hands me a small black box and says, "This will vibrate and light up when we're ready for you." It's a pager, like the ones they use at Panera Bread to let you know your order is ready.

I come back to where Tim is waiting, expectant, and tell him,

"You might as well go. I think it's going to be a while."

When they're ready to go, and I hug and kiss them both. I feel somehow like I'm the one who is leaving. "We're five minutes away," Tim says. "Just call if you want us to come back." He turns to go, and then, as if remembering something says, "Oh, so, the party? I guess..."

I nod. "Yeah," I say. "I guess you should call everyone and tell them it's off."

He kisses me again, on the forehead, before leading Caleb out the revolving door.

Alone now, I'm both more resigned to being here, and more anxious about it. It feels like the clock is ticking, like there's something I should be doing, but I don't know what. I check out the vending machines while I'm waiting, but they offer only candy bars, Life Savers, and small bags of chips, none of which is appealing at the moment. I know I need to eat something, though, and am still automatically looking for the most nutritious item, for the baby. I settle for a cellophane-sealed donut. The beverage machine has a sign that reads, "FREE COFFEE." At first I wonder if I can get decaf, since caffeine is off limits during pregnancy, but then decide it doesn't matter, I might as well have the real thing. I press the button and a small paper cup begins to fill with the thin brown liquid.

After a while my pager blinks and buzzes, and I'm told to go to a window where I am asked for my ID and insurance card. I answer questions and sign papers. When my pager blinks and buzzes again, I follow a nurse into a curtained cubicle where she asks why I'm here, and I tell her I'm having a miscarriage. The nurse's brow furrows when I mention the bleeding and she looks concerned, which I find comforting. She looks like she could be somebody's nice grandma, with grey hair, round glasses, and large bosom. It's dark and quiet in the cubicle, a little oasis in all the chaos. The nurse puts a thermometer in my mouth and asks if that was my son she saw, the one with the blond curls. I nod, surprised that anyone has been paying attention. She says he's beautiful and a sad humming sound comes from her throat, a closed-mouth sigh. I start to well up again and look away. When she puts the cuff on my arm to take my blood pressure, her hand lingers against my skin for an extra moment.

When we're done, I ask if they're going to need a urine sample because I have to go. She says yes and writes on a cup and hands it to me, along with a zip-lock bag. She says to fill the cup, put it in the bag and take it to the desk when I'm done.

In the bathroom, I see that the bleeding has started again. There's a bright red stream of it that comes out in my urine and leaves a big stain on the toilet paper. I hadn't thought to pack any pads in my bag and am relieved to find one that had been in there for months. Its pink filmy wrapper had started to come undone.

My name is called again and now a young nurse with long dark hair leads me past the blood pressure station, through a door, and further into the depths of the ER to another curtained cubicle. She leaves a gown for me to change into. A female resident comes in, and with a tentative voice asks me, "So what brings you in today?" She has my chart in her hand. I wonder if I really have to tell her, to go through it all again. Can't she just read it? I take a deep breath and say I think I'm having a miscarriage because I had some cramps last night and bleeding today. "Okay," she says. She asks me lots of questions and says, "Okay" again. She sounds stumped. After a minute she gazes toward the ceiling and whispers to herself, "What else should I ask?" To me she says, "Just a minute," and steps out of the curtains.

A while later, a different woman comes in and introduces herself as the on-call OB resident. She has freshly-applied lipstick and smiles while shaking my hand. She asks what's wrong and I tell her I'm only a few weeks pregnant and that I think I'm having a miscarriage because I had cramps last night and bleeding today.

"We'll probably want to do an ultrasound," she tells me, smiling like she's on stage in a musical. "But," she continues, and then, just like that, she disappears out of the cubicle.

I'm starting to feel a little light headed and dizzy from all the people and questions and the lights and noise. The scene has taken on an almost surreal quality, as if I'm in a postmodern theater performance and have just one line to repeat over and over. Ten minutes later, the first resident comes back in. She asks if I gave a urine sample. I tell her yes. She sticks her head into the hallway and says to someone I can't see, "She says she gave a sample...did you look on the shelf?" She steps all the way out and lowers her voice. "Well, then I don't know where it is."

Now the supervising doctor has come. He's young and handsome, with sandy hair and blue eyes. He sits down across from me, and it strikes me that he's the only one to do so; everyone else has remained standing. He asks what brings me in today, and as I tell him that I think I'm having a miscarriage because I've had some cramps and bleeding, he listens as if he already knows the story and is waiting for me to get to the punchline. When I finish, he says, "Well, the urine sample you gave shows that you are not actually pregnant." He pauses while I stare at him in shock. "Now," he says in a tone one might use with a child, "How positive was the pregnancy test you took?" He's got a grin on his face like he's got me all figured out: I'm a hysteric.

I start to panic. My mind races, retracing the circles on my temperature chart. Maybe I was wrong. Everything had been murky this month—I'd been slow to ovulate, then sure I was pregnant before I actually was. I did take one test that was negative, but that was very early on. I'd assumed it had been too soon to tell and waited to take another one. But now I wonder if that first test was right. I wonder if I misread the second, positive test. I wonder if I'm crazy, if I imagined the pregnancy. Maybe there's a mental disorder that causes women to think they're pregnant when they're not, to imagine all the symptoms and misread pregnancy tests just so they can tell their husbands the good news and then dance around the kitchen together and try out names

The doctor is waiting for an answer and I say, "I don't know—there was a plus sign."

He nods and says, "Right, right." He and the OB resident exchange glances. They're silently telling each other something, but I'm not sure what it is.

The OB resident says, "There is a slight chance that it wasn't your urine sample."

"In any case," the supervising doctor quickly says, "We want to do a blood test to see if we can't figure out what's really going on here." He stands up, making a note on my chart. "The nurse will be back in a minute to draw the sample." He's halfway through the curtain when he turns to ask if I'm feeling okay now and do I need any pain medication for my cramps.

"No," I say, realizing then that the cramps have stopped. He nods, grinning again. "Right," he says, and then steps out through the curtains.

I'm rattled now, wishing Tim were still here to help me decipher what any of this might mean. I'm not pregnant? They lost my urine sample? Both? Could I have been pregnant, but I'm not anymore? The dark-haired nurse comes in and takes some blood. She mutters to herself in a soothing tone as the tube against the inside of my elbow fills with dark red blood. When it's full, she attaches a smaller glass tube to the needle that's still in my vein and tapes it there, "In case they need more," she says. Now I've got a got a big white square on my left arm and can't really bend it. She says it'll be an hour and a half or so until they know the results. She suggests that I relax while I wait. I say I'm very thirsty and ask her for a glass of water. She says she's not sure that's okay and that she'll have to ask the doctor. She doesn't come back.

I'm left alone in the cubicle. It's about 1:00. Caleb might be up soon. I call Tim on my cell phone to give him an update. He tells me what Caleb's been doing, what he ate and how he slept, and that he's playing with the plastic parking garage my mother had bought at a garage sale. My reception starts to get spotty, and I hear him say something about having called the English Department secretary about the party. Since she had a phone list, she called everyone and told them I'd had a miscarriage, so the party was canceled. Tim apologizes, he hadn't meant for everyone to find out like that. The connection breaks.

Now I'm alone. I'm jittery from lack of food and bad coffee. I wonder what Tim's colleagues are thinking, having heard the news from the secretary. I had imagined some amount of discretion in filling people in on the details of why we were canceling the party, not an announcement about losing a pregnancy we were still surprised about ourselves. But I'm not angry, as I might have thought I'd be in this situation. I find that I'm comforted by the idea that someone out there might be feeling supportive or sympathetic towards me at the moment, even if it is some colleague of Tim's I've only met once. It occurs to me that maybe if miscarriages weren't shrouded in so much secrecy, those of us having them might get the support we really needed.

I think about having this all be over and getting released to go home, to a stack of hamburger patties in the refrigerator, colorful plasticware, and a backyard canopy. The party that never happened. I find myself wondering what we'll do with all the food

I open the novel I'd brought from home, but after reading the same sentence five times, I put it back in my bag. I try to read the celebrity gossip magazine I'd picked up in the waiting room, but it's from last year and I already know about all the scandals. I lie down on the table but I can't figure out a good position for my arm with the glass tube taped to the inside of my elbow. I feel like I'm completely disconnected from my body, but for now I want to keep it that way. This is no place to have any real feelings or to let myself wonder why this is happening. Still, my mind drifts to the long, hard bike ride Tim and I took last week while on our trip to Lake Geneva—was it too taxing? Could the half of a gin and tonic I'd had afterwards have done any damage? I can't help thinking about how long it took us to decide that we wanted a second child, that maybe my body still contained a residue of ambivalence and had been unwelcoming to this baby. I think about how easy and smooth everything had been when I was pregnant with Caleb, but maybe I'm too old now. Or maybe it's true what people say: you can only have it easy once.

After a while, I get up to wander around in the hallway, but I feel dizzy so I return to my cubicle and sit down. Finally, two and a half hours later, the supervising doctor leans his upper body though the curtains to inform me that my blood level is 10. Before he can tell me what that means, he's called away by someone in the hallway.

The OB resident comes in. She stands over me as I sit in the chair. My chart is tucked under her arm and she wrings her hands. She's nervous. Her lipstick has faded a bit, but she's smiling the same smile, a snicker like she's in church trying not to laugh. "Well," she says. "It looks as if you were pregnant, but you seem to have passed all the tissue." She takes a deep breath and says, "Sooooo." Here, she breaks into a giggle before going on to say, "There's really no need to do an ultrasound now, is there?" She gives another nervous little laugh and stares at my face.

It's clear I'm supposed to say something, but I've gotten what I came for. I've found out what I needed to know. I say, "So am I done then?"

She seems to have been expecting something else from me. She repeats what she just said, says I'll want to come in to the doctor's office on Monday or Tuesday for more blood work, to make sure I've passed all the tissue. This time, she makes imaginary quotation marks with her fingers when she says these words.

I ask if she can take the tube out of my arm. She waves her hand vaguely and says the nurse will be in soon to do that. She goes on about taking more blood and gives me a card with the number on it to call. Bending to point to each digit as she says it, she reads the number to me and then looks into my face to see that I'm comprehending her. "I'd like to go now," I say and reach into my bag for my phone.

She seems disappointed, like I was supposed to want more from her. "Well, we'll get your paperwork going," she says and slips out.

I call Tim to tell him what's going on, but the reception is bad. I hear him saying, "What? What?" and then, "I'm just going to come."

I don't really know what's supposed to happen now or what I'm waiting for, other than the nurse to come back and take this thing out of my arm. I have to get out of here now. I change my clothes, trying not to catch the tube that's still taped to my arm on my shirt as I pull it over my head. I pick up my bag. I want out. It's over, and I can feel, now, everything from the day beginning to rise inside my chest.

I'm pacing in the hallway outside my cubicle. No one comes. The dark-haired nurse looks up from across the desk and looks away, like a waitress with too many tables who doesn't want to know that I need more coffee.

Finally, as I turn toward the direction I'd been brought in from, I keep walking. I am going to walk out of here. My heart is pounding with the possibility, and I feel my legs powered by adrenaline as they carry me down the corridor, but when I get to the end of the hall, I'm faced with an emergency door and an "Alarm Will Sound" sign. I feel dizzy and defeated. I turn back to where my cubicle was, but instead of stopping, I continue in the other direction. I'm really leaving. It's against the rules, but I don't care and I'll rip this tube out of my own arm, at home. I ask a nurse wearing jazzy, multi-colored scrubs how to get out, and she tells me to take a right at the end of the hallway. I say thank you very much and follow where she had pointed. When I make the turn, I see a door, and through the window in the door, I can see the driveway. Outside. I can feel the release even before I push the door open, and I walk out into the afternoon sun.

As I march past the security guard, I see Tim's car at the end of the driveway. He's just pulling in. I need to get to him. I start to run. As I feel myself rushing down the small hill that leads to the parking lot, I hear the security guard behind me, saying "Ma'am. Ma'am!" He's running after me now. I only want to get to Tim. The guard stops me, his hand on my shoulder. "Ma'am," he says, his voice surprisingly gentle. "It's illegal for you to leave with that thing in your arm."

"But I'm fine," I say. "I can take it out at home." The guard steps in front of me, blocking the sidewalk. "That's my husband right there," I say, waving my arm in the direction of Tim's car. I'm looking around the guard's body. "He can take it out. We'll just go. I'm fine." My voice sounds ragged and frantic. By now Tim has seen me and the guard waves him over. I let my bag drop to the ground and my shoulders curl forward as I feel myself start to crumple. A sob escapes from my body, and Tim's arms are around me. The guard takes a step away from us and lets us have this.

"Just take me home," I say into Tim's chest, but I know I've lost.

"She needs to go back in to have that thing removed," the guard says. He is apologetic. "Why don't you go on in with her and I'll park the car for you," he says. I stand on the sidewalk crying while Tim gets Caleb out of the car. He gives the guard the key and says thank you. I take Caleb who looks confused by my tears, but smiles anyway. Tim puts his arm around me and the three of us walk back up the hill.

Inside, I am readmitted. There is new paperwork to fill out and

I have to present my insurance card again. When the woman asks me the reason for my visit, I point to my arm and say, "I have to have this tube removed." She looks confused, so I add, "I need to be discharged."

Threads
Linda A. Vandlac Smith

Only this morning
I lay cramped
by your anger
clinging to
the feeble threads
of flawed love
in my womb.

Nature sides with you
rejects imperfections.
My thighs weep red
muscles twitch
out of control.

By afternoon
tears leave me
sterile of emotion.
Who can fault god
for this cloudless day
birds' bright banter
or the red geranium
you bring for an apology?

As you mouth
your careful regret
the moment snags
words drop like buttons
at loose ends
bounce toward silence.

Outside the world
still breathes. I
watch a spider's web
through the window
a frozen cartwheel
hanging on anchored
only by threads.

breathe
out

Counterpoint
Carol Barrett

My six-year-old has saved a gray mouse,
out of the cat's mouth like a fish
hook, his ears small gills
in her hands. He had pawed it
all across the rug, claw-pricks
she wet with a bowl of water
from her play kitchen. *I holded him*
on my chest and he didn't run away!
Those tiny beats thrumming her heart,
shuddering the space between there
and now.

    *

My daughter cannot know how I too
have kept awake for a thumping
faster than my own beat minding
the hours, how I have charted
the dipping frequency of thumb-print
kicks, irregularities in pitch
and tone, hearts like a tandem
bicycle, *lub-dup lub-dup* underlying
pum-bum pum-bum pum-bum pum-bum.
She cannot know how I have memorized
this music precisely, point
by counterpoint, felt the cool
mask of oxygen as rhythm rearranged
itself, the quick beat slowing almost

to a match, disappearing in fog,
resuming like a train around a bend,
the nurses' faces pretending to hide
what they know, the way they signal
each other with minimum alarm,
the staccato pianissimo of code words,
a gurney arriving in my room, one
side split down in a split-second.

*

I imagine this the same ecstasy of nuns
in summer rain, habits fluttering like peach
blossoms in the wind, or of a hailstorm
in the middle of Kansas that keeps
coming, and coming, yes
the ecstasy of a congregation
of crickets, of ferris wheels
rocking the sky blue
and blue, of ferns unfurling
their long slow curls, of the first
grass knot tied for the first doll.

*

My daughter knows only that she hid
the mouse in the hall closet,
imagines him still there, rumpling
winter scarves and mittens, building
a mouse house with play kitchen,
a jungle gym made of hangers and old ties.
She imagines he is forever safe
in the world, this very moment

nestled in, watching the latest
little mouse video, munching popcorn.

*

As I imagine *pum-bum pum-bum*
my little girl, my thimble-
hearted baby, forever breathing.

Only Children
Elise Blackwell

my husband is the tenth of fifteen children—the first eleven are biological, and the final four adopted. His father is an obstetrician. His eldest sister has eight kids. Most of his siblings have three or five kids, or at least two.

I am the only offspring of divorced parents. My father is an only child. My mother has one sibling she prefers to avoid. Holidays are small. The group activity is a coffee tray and the interminable "sit and visit" that leads experienced relatives to disappear to recessed rooms with any available book or the claim of a migraine, which leads visitors to sympathize with the victims of slow torture.

Holidays at my in-laws' ranch are pan-continental games. Around eleven, maybe even ten, one of my husband's sisters—the one who was the "good one," homecoming queen, virgin on her wedding night—pulls out the Old Mr. Boston guide, opens it at random, and mixes up pitchers of something or another. One Easter it was gin daisies; one Thanksgiving it was mint juleps. Packs of children build forts on their fast way to feral. They aren't allowed inside before dinner unless they are bleeding more profusely than a band-aid handed through a crack in the door will staunch. They urinate al fresco in the eucalyptus grove that supplies what firewood a San Diego hacienda needs. The men wrap whole animals—a calf, a pig, a lamb once named Tina—in banana leaves. Buried in smoldering pits, the meat slow-cooks all afternoon. The many dogs linger close. Volleyball is played; horseshoes thrown. Whole baseball and water polo teams are fielded. The kids' games end in a draw, but competitive brothers run up scores in the grown-up games. Those children, too old for wildness, practice parts for the after-dinner play they will perform on the spotlighted front lawn. Just before it's time to eat, younger children strip to be washed down with the fire hose. After dinner, after stacks of dishes, after the play, guitars come out, as well as an accordion, and sometimes a fiddle. The voices are passable, and everyone knows the words to the same songs.

I fell in love with my husband before I knew his family, but I may have married him to be part of it. That was before the fractures and factions were visible, before the divorces and disorders, and before everyone knew the ugly things that only some had known before. But those are part of a different story—one that isn't mine to tell.

ON THE eve of marriage, I was newly twenty-five. My grandmother sat me down and told me that I was getting a nice husband, and told me to be nice him. "What about how he treats me?" I asked. After she made it clear that it wasn't his temperament that had her worried, she added: "But don't you mind what the Pope or his parents have to say. You wait, and don't have too many. Children are nice and all that, but they're not really that great."

My husband's family celebrated our marriage. With fifteen children—six of them male—no son had sired a son. Not a single grandson bore the family name. "You're going to have the first Bajo boy," I was told. Depending on who said it, the words held joy, awe, envy bordering on hatred, and the weight of fact.

We started trying to conceive on our wedding night. Though I would get pregnant over and over and over, there were a couple of miscarriages, but most of the pregnancies—all ectopic—ended in emergency surgery.

Dozens of times, my mother-in-law said this: "Fertile Myrtle, that's what I am. Daddy'd pee across the street and I'd get knocked up." A sister-in-law laughed, "We're so fucking fertile." *My words exactly*, I thought.

The one sister in nine who struggled to conceive yielded two daughters. "You know," my mother-in-law whispered of her seventh child's need for medical assistance, "I think her husband picked up something in a port-of-call and passed it along, if you know what I mean." Everyone knew what she meant.

I suspect family stories. I come from a part of the south where revision is a pastime practiced over the first round of whiskey sours. My family can redefine a cousin's suicide attempt as a "misunderstanding," a lesbian lover as a "babysitter." I knew that my sister-in-law's difficulties had nothing to do with venereal infection. Like mine, her appendix has been removed just in the nick of time. Yet people hold contradictory beliefs every day. Some members of my husband's family believed the innuendo even as they understood the content was false.

My appendix had started to rupture in a college karate class. It was misdiagnosed for hours because the pain was in my back. One doctor asked me if I was sexually active. "Check my white-cell count," I winced. Appendicitis runs in my family. It killed my great-grandmother, and almost got my cousin. When the surgeons finally dove in, they found the small offender hiding behind my colon. The peritonitis could have killed me. Instead it left my abdominal cavity webbed with adhesions that protected my internal organs, possibly saved my life, and doomed most of my would-be babies.

Four days after one of my ectopic surgeries, I struggled to walk up the nearest little hill. Stapled together hip bone to hip bone but eschewing the pain medication that left me unable to hold down food or write coherent sentences, I wondered what was being said about me and wished I didn't care.

ONE SUMMER a family calendar was planned, and a photographer enlisted. Each married child would get a page with his or her family. The younger, single children would share the final page. I was pleased that my husband and I were granted a whole month, and that we were considered a family. Our dog, ever alert for a stationary victim, sat next to us for petting. The dog and I had chosen each other at the pound. I had changed her name from Penny to Finney, because my husband disapproves of dogs named after people and, smart dog, she recognized the rhyme. As the photographer snapped our picture, a sister-in-law called out: "Finney can't be your child."

I was stupid or masochistic enough to request the pathology report on the first "products of ectopic." It was male, by all measures normal but stuck in a scarred-up pipe. The first Bajo boy, I thought. The third baby grew to the size of a walnut, stretching my tube to the point of rupture before the blood leaking into my abdomen hurt severely enough to send me, doubled over, to the doctor. As with the appendix, I waited almost too long.

WE TRIED to adopt. I think Wanless came between pregnancies number two and three, but it might have been between three and four. Wanless's mother was gone. His father was in prison forever. The foster parents were divorcing. His foster mother knew about my father-in-law. She knew about the infants he delivered for a jar of pennies, the pregnant women he sheltered even when it meant telling off or paying off a meth-dealing boyfriend. The foster mother was concerned, she said, about the little boy and about me. *Who talks about me?*, I wondered. But I smiled thinking that the first Bajo boy might be named Wanless.

Not quite three, Wanless spoke no English and scant Spanish. The day I met him, he picked up a piece of crumpled paper from the floor and carried it until he found a trash can. We spent time with him, made him snacks, changed his diaper, and played. He was beautiful in the way we think all kids are, but only a few truly are. A lawyer friend cautioned me: "never return him sunburned." I stocked up on sunblock and bought a small hat with a wide brim. After a few weeks, I called the adoption agency. The case-worker believed that Wanless's foster parents were poised to adopt him, and didn't know they were bust. I was being used for free childcare while they collected support money.

The alarmed man told me—with the brutality and kindness of swift honesty—that we would never adopt Wanless, who was half Mexican. First choice: a biethnic couple. Second choice: a Mexican-American couple. Me: not a chance in hell. I spoke with anger but, for at least once in my life, with the best of intentions: "Find him a home before he turns three. Don't condemn him." I phoned more than once.

When I heard that Wanless was placed with a teacher and his wife, I was glad for him and happy that I had been decent. When I heard they might change his name, I was sad. I couldn't think of a name that rhymed with Wanless.

My husband dwelled on the troubles that can accompany even a successful adoption. His younger adopted brother had devel-oped schizophrenia in his early twenties, disappeared for a year, and was found only when the newspaper published a photo of homeless men waiting in line for winter shelter. Just as disturb-ing to my husband was the adopted sister who declined college tuition and maintains a seemingly inherited taste for chili-mac, fruit cocktail cake, and peanut butter pie. But those are excuses; the truth is that Wanless broke our heart. Our marriage would have been next. We never again tried to adopt.

THE FIFTH pregnancy was a debacle. A misread sonogram sug-gested a regular pregnancy, but a danger of miscarriage. I laid down for a week, crossed my legs, and prayed to everything. Then the bad news, the real news came: it had never been all right. Surgery was scheduled for the next day. The doctor said, in an admirably straightforward tone, that it was time to take both fallopian tubes. Both had already been cut open and sewn back together. One now bulged with yet another would-be, a comic fraction of an inch from a good chance at life. It was time to stop. The surgery, because it would leave me barren, was moved to a non-Catholic hospital.

My doctor apologized later as I wept, and said that the tube without the pregnancy hadn't looked totally shot. He was sorry; he just couldn't take it. After ten years of trying, he and his wife had recently adopted. I felt condemned to yet another ectopic in the future, one more scar with a name as pretty as Cora Grace. I wrote a vicious letter, considered refusing to pay, trashed the letter, and wrote angry checks to doctor, hospital, pathologist, and anesthesiologist, just to be done with them.

WE'D BEEN told that we were good candidates for in vitro fertilization. We conceived readily; it was just that the babies got stuck. Like adoption, we didn't pursue it. We were broke and sick of doctors, but we had abstract reasons as well. As the daughter of two evolutionary biologists, I understood the implications of bypassing natural selection. I couldn't stand the idea that any of my fertilized eggs might be destroyed, and I believed that certain expenditures are sins in the world as it is. These were personal sentiments, not considered opinions, and most certainly not political decisions. As such—and because I cheered friends procreating however they could—I applied them only to myself. And this is also part of the truth: there was much more to my life, at least between the dramas, than only children.

One of the ectopics was mercifully timed: I came home from the hospital the day March Madness started. I had a television back then and, a basketball fanatic, I watched every game of the NCAA championships while I recuperated. It was the year that

Princeton coach Pete Carrill called for the backdoor pass that knocked UCLA out of the tournament. Childlessness makes writing time easier to come by, and money less essential. My work got better. I took to exercise with true vengeance, punishing the body that had failed me into fabulous shape. My husband and I threw parties and went out a lot. My father-in-law—when he caught us on the way to an afternoon movie or late-night concert—told us that everything would change when we had kids. The first few times, these words pulled tears. Later I just said, "I know, but we don't." Once in awhile I was even glad that we didn't.

We traveled and liked it. We determined to be expatriate writers in Mexico, live on the cheap, and do things people with children don't. We were leaning toward the gracious city of Colima, but decided to look at Michoacán before deciding. Self-absorbed, we forgot about the tourist draw of the Day of the Dead, and after our first week, found ourselves with no place to stay in the three towns we tried. My stomach was empty and still unsteady after a run-in with bad mayonnaise. A sympathetic clerk told us to strike out for Angahuan, to the cabins people stay in to view or climb Paricutin, the volcano that slowly buried a city in 1941. No seasonal tourists would be there, he assured us. We found it, rented a cabin, slept well, woke up, and hiked the volcano—seven hours round trip over the sharp lava beds. My bootless ankles were cut to bleeding. Still unable to eat and now pounds down, I had to hold my pants up with my hands. Back at the cabin, I took the best shower of my life and changed shoes. We walked into the tiny town and assembled a meal from the soon-to-close market's offering of canned tuna, carrots, hot sauce, and tortillas. The owner's little boy apologized as he handed us the soft warm tortillas. "I'm sorry they are homemade. We sold out of the others." My appetite was back; the food was sublime.

It was the night before the Dead of the Dead, the night on which dead children— los angelitos—are said to visit. The walled cemetery was lush with marigolds. Toys and pictures and candies adorned the smallest graves. The Americans swarming Pátzcuaro and Janitzio would have said "how authentic," but there were no other Americans in Angahuan. Besides us and four German college students, everyone was local. Few spoke fluent Spanish, and we could not speak their older language. But we understood when to accept shots of mescal offered from the little silver trays some men chained around their necks. I remembered my grandfather's admonition: "Never drink homemade liquor. You'll go blind." I'd survived the white lightening sighted, so I persevered.

It might have been the following night. It might have been a few days later. But I tell myself that my daughter was conceived that night—on La Noche de los Niños Muertos. We did not move to Mexico.

When my father-in-law found out I was carrying a girl, his words were: "What the hell's the matter with you?" He was joking, sort of, but he had to recover lying down. The miracle baby would not be the first Bajo boy.

Everyone was cautious. Every backache I mentioned was followed by prescriptions of immediate rest. But the pregnancy was healthy. I exercised and glowed and gained the recommended weight to the pound. After seven months, showers were thrown. "Sarah is a good strong name," said my mother-in-law. Her name is Sarah. Her first child's name is Sarah. Her first grandchild's name is Sarah. Several other of her grandchildren live under the name Sarah.

I GAVE birth in exquisite pain and named my child Esme Claire. She was angelic for several days.

When the colic set in, Esme screamed for several hours every evening. She cried most other times as well. She never seemed happy and never slept more than three hours straight. I believed that she was in physical pain, but could do little more than nurse her, walk her, and sing the only songs I knew the lyrics to: "Angel from Montgomery," "Amazing Grace," and "Carmelita." My mother-in-law—who had been named mother of the year three times—could not calm her. My daughter would not be cuddled. The single babysitting disaster concluded when I found the two of them matching wills over a pacifier, Esme winning with the final spit and glare. "I had easy babies," my mother-in-law said, "You don't." The babysitting offers ended.

When my mother-in-law converted to her husband's religion, she adopted not only the Catholicism, but its peculiar Old World variant, replete with pictures of Jesus' bleeding heart and superstitions beyond the imagination of any Portuguese fishwife. My happy ending turned perverse for her. I was never supposed to have a baby, family members whispered. The baby was flaccid, was exhibiting signs of diabetes, had autism, or was mentally retarded. A sister-in-law called from 2,000 miles away. She was worried about our state of denial, and assured us that parenting a handicapped child could be enriching. Another relative gave me a copy of that horribly trite essay comparing life with a disabled child to a trip to Holland when your heart was set on Paris: "You wanted to see the Eiffel Tower, but windmills are nice too."

The pediatrician reassured me: "Your baby isn't the one who has something wrong with her head." Friends comforted me with statistics about colic.

We moved far away. We gave assorted reasons but, really, there was only one. We took great financial risk (and, for a long while, loss) so that our daughter would grow up where no one would tell her that something was wrong with her. At three, she was a party draw, taking all comers in chess, and beating not just nine-year-olds, but their parents. I eavesdropped when my husband told his parents that, due to her high intelligence, Esme was entering a program for gifted children. It shouldn't have mattered so much to me. As much as we pretend we don't care what our families think, we usually do.

On days when I felt mean in every sense of the word, I hoped that the first Bajo boy would materialize out of wedlock. But there is still no Bajo boy. Two years ago, my husband's youngest sister, the final adopted child, gave birth to a baby girl. Her name is Lauren Elise; the middle name is mine. I wish that I could meet her, but I cannot go there again.

My daughter cheered up when she learned to walk, but she's still moody, and sometimes downright cranky. She adores older children, begs for a baby sister, and despises being an only child as much as I did. After all, only a sibling knows how strange your parents really are, and in which ways. I lost five pregnancies before my daughter was born, and one after. Flush with the optimism of recent success, I believed in the last one. I believed I would have another girl and named her Cora Grace. Esme made that one harder and easier—easier because I had a baby to go home to, and harder because I really knew what I had just lost. "Even a baby brother, if that's all I can get," my daughter negotiates. I never tell her: "It would have been a sister. Her name was Cora Grace." People say that Esme would do well in a large family, and they are right. She lives as an only child, but she is also—if only to me—the sixth of seven. I plan to take her to Angahuan someday, to hike the volcano if she wants to.

Stillbirth
Barbara Crooker

She said, "Your daughters
are so beautiful.
One's a copper penny,
the other's a chestnut colt."
But what about
my first daughter,
stillborn
at term,
cause
unknown?

Ten years later
and I sift the ground
for clues: what was
it I did?
Guilt is part
of my patchwork;
grief folds me up
like an envelope.

In the hospital,
the doctors turned
their eyes, told me
not to leave
my room.
But I heard them,
those babies in the night,
saw women from Lamaze

in the corridor.
They would be wheeled home
with blossoms & blankets,
while I bled the same,
tore the same,
and came home, alone.

Later,
women showered me
with stories
of babies lost:
to crib death,
   abortion,
   miscarriage;
   lost;
   the baby
   that my best friend
   gave up at fourteen.

They wouldn't let me hold her:
all I saw were glimpses:
   a dark head,
   a doll's foot,
   skin like a bruise,
They wouldn't let me name her,
         or bury her,
         or mourn her.

Ten years later
and I do not have
the distance:
I carry her death
like an egg
in my pocket.

Writing Around the Word
Julie Danho

In your letter, not one comma is mis-
placed, not one phrase hangs
mid-air. Everything is here
but the word. I look up

synonyms—*misfire, mischance,*
meet with disaster—not one
of which you use. Why,
out of a crowd, did its prefix choose

you, latch onto your hand
as if lost? You write how,
that morning on the train,
you'd auditioned names, never

sensed you'd been left. You have
nothing now to bury
but the word. Following your
need, I want to let it fall

back down my throat.
But since I know this grief
thrives in silence, splits
and multiplies until

it presses on your chest
through the night, let me cup
my hands beneath your mouth,
and catch whatever slides out.

Early Sorrow
Elizabeth Dougherty Dolan

After the three sisters had waited nine months
for the baby who was born dead,
they fretted about her being buried alone.
So they placed next to her
their almost-favorite stuffed animals,
the toucan by her plump cheeks
and the kookaburra by her elbow.
In her hands, they put the board book
Good Night Gorilla, in which the gorilla-hero steals
the keys from the zookeeper's belt,
and frees the armadillo and hyena.
The sisters knew she would laugh
when the animals followed the keeper to his house,
and the gorilla slept in his bed.
Plus she would learn about locks and keys.
And when Grandma died seven days later,
they knew she would read the book to the baby
and blow on her belly and sing
Toora, Loora, Loora.
These are the things
the three sisters did and told us,
the grown ups who did nothing, but sit
like stones in our chairs, staring.

Some Call It Luck
R.G. Evans

Planetary alignments, perhaps, let you have a child,
the cosmos saying *We absolve you your degradation,*
we allow you a little future at last.

Some nights, you try to share the optimism,
to believe your grave is half empty, not half full.
Some nights, like this one:

you remember the blood
the foreign feel of your wife's hand
when the ER doc said miscarriage.

With your family asleep all around you, save the one
who never made it here, it doesn't sound too wrong,
somehow, when no one can hear you say it—*lucky*—

so you say it again.

Long After the Loss
Maureen Tolman Flannery

They made an unspoken pact
to bury grief somewhere in the house
where the throaty sound of laughter still jumped out
from behind a doorway at unexpected times
to grab the ankles of their recovery.

The pain itself was hard in the center,
but sticky to the touch and gray-fuzzed on the surface
like a piece of fruit long forgotten in the bottom
of a bag of important papers.

Sometimes she would find it
under a clean stack of folded towels
or, reaching for the right spice, she might
touch it in the back of a pantry cupboard.

It caught him off guard in a tool chest
near the tack hammer half the size of the one he was using.

Mostly they just stuck the grief
back into another place
and went on their way of a hobbled day
as if running a three-legged race
in which they kept falling down together.
But sometimes one of them would take it up
and try to know it better,
like a curious old acquaintance
or hold onto it tightly

through the spores and mold-dust
and try to toss it out of the house.

The Continuum
Jesse Loren

It was this way,
disconnecting cables, then
analyzing the row of tubers grown in the yard...
She called them hearts,
said they always come from the garden.

Then it was time.
To erase all the crayon drawings of rectangular houses
with parallelogram roofs
along right triangles and small squares of chimneys
which
grew circuitous smoke like love folding back on
itself.

She was difficult from birth, and this way,
disconnecting the cables, we were ready
to put her tuber under the ground.

Miscarriage
Gail Lukasik

light resists itself
trees & houses hold
deep shadows

all day it is twilight
so sleep never comes
yet waited for

the playground fallow
the vapor streetlights
a soft confusion of purpose

clouds seize smoke & smog
as if breeding their own loss

once again water resembles
its blank surface
where objects are
assumed
not seen

& grief a color
I wear on my sleeve
as I tuck myself inside
one arm at a time

Wrapping
Stephen Mead

the dead baby, a cold burn
for a minute, then white duck nappies
changed, the blanket folding over, tucked
eloquent, a wool cocoon with room for
the head, the fingers, life's dignified
casing.
They say, "Forget it, have ano..."
They say... awkward, apologetic,
and of course we understand.
There's no adequate etiquette
without tripping maudlin, heavy
on the violins, or switching subjects briskly.
Yet, in utero, premature, after six months
of expectation, suddenly, say, a grey
pigeon feather, lying flat across the screen
and a consoling hand on the cheek
as opposed to an Alpha Centauri wail.
Still, loss is born, so it must not
be a dream, bad, forgettable. The body
knows, having carried, held pictures, a triptych
now ripped at its hinges or, no, not ripped,
rather bound quite invisibly, as if at a distance...
So we and our child travel

White Birds
Dinty W. Moore

*t*ommy Prendergast is in my kitchen, scratching his bald spot and talking up a storm. He seems to be having an argument with someone, only Tommy is alone in the room. My refrigerator door is wide open and cold air is pouring out. The back door is open too, and I'm standing outside, about to walk in.

When I do, Tommy says hello and goes right on talking as if I've been there with him all along. He's wearing a blue nylon jogging outfit, and the skin on his face is red from the sun.

"I saw these girls," he says, holding his hand up the way you do to show how tall someone is. "They're about twelve years old and skinny. You know how I mean, don't you Daniel?"

"Close the refrigerator," I say, "or take something out of it."

He looks surprised, but ignores my suggestion. "Three girls. I'm looking at them, and I notice they're looking at these birds. You know, the big white ones."

"Egrets," I say.

"Yeah, egrets. Over at the lake."

A large lake borders the Garden District of Baton Rouge, and that, I suppose, is where Tommy got the sunburn. The lake is about the size of an airport and the egrets use it like one, gliding in and out according to some schedule only they seem to understand. So far, I'm pretty much following what Tommy is trying to say.

"So the girls are watching the birds?"

"Right, right. They're just watching, and I'm just watching

them, and that's when it happened."

"What happened?"

He grabs a can of Old Milwaukee, shuts the refrigerator, and finally sits down at the table. "Never mind," he says, "it's nothing." He drains the can and drops his head forward as if he's fallen asleep.

Tommy has been my friend since we were eight, someone I was always glad to see crawling over the fence into my patch of backyard. He was much littler than other kids our age, but made up for it by being somewhat fearless. Now, at thirty, he's still a small man, but balding, with a faint moustache. He's a good carpenter, but has never managed to hold a steady job. I've seen his falling asleep act before, more often than I like to admit, so I simply go to the refrigerator, pull out another beer, and set it in front of him.

"The girls," I say. "Tell me."

He looks around, confused. "Daniel, how'd you get here?"

"Just tell me about the girls."

"The girls?"

Playing dumb is another of Tommy's favorite games and probably the main reason I'm the only friend he has left.

"Get to the point," I say. "Tell me what you have to tell me or give me the beer back and get out."

He sits up straight and looks me in the eye. "While I was watching these girls, they floated across the water. Then they turned into white birds."

WHEN MY wife Laura left me, Tommy was nearly as upset as I was about her leaving. Laura took Tommy seriously, while everyone else in town treated him like a bad joke.

She left because of the baby, or specifically, because there was no baby. We married just last October, when I got my job at the library, and we decided to have a child right away. It was her idea, but I didn't fight it. She was pregnant by Christmas and so happy she would sit for hours propped up in bed, just smiling, like a girl with a secret that she loved turning over in her mind. Laura was as content and as beautiful as I'd ever seen anyone be.

Until mid-February. There was no warning. Just cramps in the middle of the night and the baby was gone within an hour.

I told her not to worry, we'd get over it. But more than just a baby flowed out of Laura that morning. Her whole life seemed to float away. She no longer smiled at anything. She no longer wanted to see our friends. She didn't want to talk. She was twenty-four and had plenty of years to try again, but she didn't want that either.

"We can have another baby," I'd say.

"I don't want another baby," Laura would answer. "I want my baby."

To Laura, the baby was as real as if she had held it in her arms before it died. To me, it was never really anything at all. And somehow she didn't seem able to forgive me for that.

Last month, she moved to New Orleans for the summer, to be with her sister in the big house on Prytania. And to be away from me.

THE TUESDAY that I come home to find Tommy standing by my refrigerator and talking to himself, he ends up sleeping on my couch. He keeps drinking my beer and repeating the story about the three girls turning into white birds, and eventually he is too drunk to walk the half mile back to his apartment.

I wake up Wednesday morning to see Tommy, dripping wet and wrapped in a blue towel, sitting on the corner of my bed. "I've been thinking of killing myself," he says.

I pretend I don't hear. You can't stop Tommy from being difficult, but there's no need to encourage him either. He's often talked of suicide, and there are days I reach a point where I wish he'd just shut up and try.

"Let's talk," he insists. "Let's talk right now."

"I'm sleeping. This can wait."

He shakes his head. "No. It can't."

I look at him and realize he might be serious. Something in his eyes hints that, something in the way they don't flinch when he says the word "No." I sit up, put on my glasses, and walk to the kitchen. He follows.

"I don't believe you," I say, "but tell me, for the sake of argument, why you're going to kill yourself?" I turn my back on him deliberately and start the water for coffee.

"Because of you know what."

"No, what?" I ask, folding a paper towel into a triangle because I've run out of filters.

"You know."

I turn, and he is pointing in the direction of the lake, like someone might point to a room where an insane relative has been locked away for years. Then he says, "You know, the doctor says I can't have children. He says I'm sterile as a fresh needle."

"You aren't even married," I mumble back.

"It's all the same. I can't have kids, right? So there's no point in getting married. So there's no point in going out with women. So why even bother trying to find a date? So why live, huh Daniel?" He laughs, then goes to my refrigerator and nonchalantly helps himself to some juice.

I finish making the coffee, confused by this latest bit of silliness, and end up thinking about Laura and how she would have taken Tommy much more seriously. Tommy hadn't dated anyone for six years, but she would have listened to Tommy and found a way to help him out. Most people treat Tommy like a stupid adult, but Laura always treated him like a bright child.

All I can do is what I can do, though, and some days it's all I can do just to put up with Tommy. While I'm thinking this, Tommy looks up at me like he's suddenly realized something important.

"You're right," he says. "It's no reason to kill myself."

"Good," I answer, cracking an egg into a bowl. "Let's have breakfast."

When the fried eggs and toast are ready, I make Tommy tell me again what he saw at the lake, and I try forcing him to be specific. It's something I remember my father doing with me.

"The girls just lift off the bank," Tommy explains. "They float, Daniel. They float like angels, right out to the cypress."

"What do you mean, they float?"

"I mean above the water."

"How far above the water?"

"About two feet. They float straight out, and there's some sort of smoke around them."

"Smoke?"

"Like fog or something, but the sun's shining."

"Okay. Then what?"

"They turn into birds."

"What kind of birds?"

"The white ones. I told you that already."

He seems excited, but not puzzled. It's as if he doesn't realize this is impossible, as if he thinks he's seen something rare but totally reasonable. Once, years back, Tommy told me he'd been treated for depression. Later he said it was schizophrenia—but he often changes facts like that, on a whim. Another night, when we'd been drinking, Tommy told me he would sometimes hallucinate, that it scared him a little, but that he basically liked it. I didn't know then whether to believe him or not.

"How do you know you didn't imagine this," I ask, back at the breakfast table. "How do you know you really saw the girls turn into birds?"

"I saw it."

"You hallucinate, Tommy. You told me. How do you know you didn't hallucinate this?"

He gets up from the table, walks around to my side, and stands right over me, looking as serious as I've ever seen him.

"It wasn't like that. I know the difference, and it wasn't like that at all."

I CAN be foolish at times, and make mistakes, but I look at practical people and they don't seem to be doing much better. So even though Tommy's story is preposterous, I say that I believe him. And when he says he wants to learn more about the birds, to spend evenings at the lake and observe them at close range, I agree to go along. My life hasn't been proceeding so well with me in charge, so how could it hurt to let Tommy dictate things for a while?

We get to lake about the time the sun starts to lower itself toward the I-10 overpass. I watch the sun, and Tommy watches the birds. One night, our third, a large egret appears in front of us, so large that I assume it's a male. He swoops in, banking to a wide turn and tilting his wings sharply. For a moment, he appears to be suspended in mid-air, then quickly he stretches his neck and glides to a landing.

Standing in about six inches of water, he draws his wings tight around his body and pulls back his long neck, until he's only half the size he seemed in flight. I glance toward Tommy, and the look on his face reminds me for a moment of the way he would look when we were boys exploring this same lake. I'm glad to see that. I look back at the bird and wonder if he ever worries like we do, if lost children and lost wives ever cause him to lose any sleep.

But the white bird just stands in the shallow water, not letting on to what he's thinking. His eyes scan the surface, his thin legs remain fixed in a firm V. Then, without warning, his neck darts forward like a rubber band and he snares a three-inch minnow in his orange beak, swallowing it whole. I can see the lump slowly work down his slender neck, a quarter-inch at a time. Then, he turns and looks at me, his head at an odd angle, as if perhaps he has something to say but can't find the words. That's silly, of course, but it seems that way for the moment. Finally, his wings slap the water and he flies off toward a cypress about twenty yards out in the lake.

WHEN WE return to my apartment that night, Tommy stands on my sofa in his bare feet and pretends to be an egret. "Do you have any idea how hard it is to catch a fish? Did you ever try to grab a fish?" he keeps asking.

I assure him that catching a fish by hand, or beak, is not easy.

"And things look different under water," he says, his neck moving from side to side, his eyes patrolling my living room carpet for imaginary minnows. "You look through the water at a fish and it's not really where you think it is."

"Light refraction."

"That's it. Refraction. Birds have to adjust for that. They have to understand physics."

I suggest to Tommy that egrets don't need to understand physics, that they just know instinctively where to strike. Tommy won't hear of it.

"How do you know? How do you know? You don't know what a bird knows and what he doesn't."

He seems about to get angry, so I concede the point.

A FEW weeks later, Tommy moves in with me. "Closer to the lake," he says, but I know the truth, which is that his landlady has tossed him out. He's not sleeping much now, and he's becoming harder and harder to talk to.

The night he moves in, an oppressively hot Friday evening, I ask him again to tell me about his vision. I'm looking for a clue, some key to what is happening. Tommy repeats lucidly and without significant change the story of the three skinny girls staring into the water, then floating like ghosts out into the lake. But when I quiz him, trying to poke a hole in his delusion, he doesn't want to talk.

"It's not important," he says.

"Of course it is," I argue. "You wouldn't have seen it if it weren't important."

"Forget it."

"Why aren't you interested? Why don't you want to know what it means?" I ask.

"Daniel," he says, reversing roles, seeming as exasperated with me as I always am with him.

"What?"

"I was hallucinating. Just drop it."

Tommy is still fascinated by the birds, hiking day and night out to the lake, but the vision seems to have merely become something that brought him there—like a movie he saw, found interesting, and forgot about a week later. All he cares about now is understanding the birds, and in his own way he probably can. Like them, he spends hours sitting quietly by the lake, watching nature at nature's pace. He differs from the birds in that he cannot fly, and in that he returns to my apartment every night to share the six pack of beer I buy. But to the extent that a bird thinks, I suppose he's thinking like one. A bird just wants to catch enough fish to live. Tommy just wants to see enough birds.

Something about the three skinny girls and the white birds continues to fascinate me, though, despite Tommy's change of mind. As a youngster, I dreamed of flight and exotic lands, and these birds know both. The girls make me think of Laura, too, and of how delicate she turned out to be. In the weeks before she left, she seemed unable to speak, unable to say what was on her mind. Like the egret that night, the one that stared into my eyes and cocked its head as if wondering how to make its point.

THE FINAL night I spend along the water with Tommy is in early August. He's still living on my couch and I'm still trying to put it all together, to make sense of what is happening to Tommy.

It feels like rain, so we grab our sandwiches and drive to the lake in my car. We're sitting quietly on the bank as dusk settles in, Tommy watching a tree full of white birds and me worrying about Tommy, when he catches me off guard.

"Why don't you call Laura?"

I don't answer right away. I just look across the water. I called every other night for a while, when she first moved out, but we ended up either fighting or sitting quietly, not knowing what to say. At the end of every call, I would ask her to quit being depressed and she would tell me to quit saying that.

"You should call her," Tommy says. "It's not right."

"Let's talk about something else."

"You must think about her."

"No, not really."

"You're lying. I know. You think about her all the time. You should call her, make her come back. What if I weren't here? Who would be your friend?"

I should pick up on that comment maybe, be more concerned about what Tommy means, but I'm worrying more about myself. "She doesn't care about me," I say.

"You didn't care about her. She wanted you to love the baby like she did, and you didn't. You know that's why she left."

"I don't know what I know anymore."

"Well, I do, and I think you're acting dumb."

"Why is this any of your business?" I ask, but I know he's right. I know that I need to keep calling Laura, or I will lose her, but knowing and doing are two entirely different things. I almost say to Tommy that I have no idea what to tell Laura when I call, but I notice he's watching an egret that has landed very near us, closer than any egret has dared land before. The bird is particularly beautiful, the eyes soft and distant, the white body thinner and more immaculate than other egrets I've seen. I can't tell really, but I can guess, so I guess this one is a female. She rolls her neck slowly, as if tired and trying to remember something. Then she spots Tommy, and stares at him.

I'm watching her, wondering whether it's easier to be a bird than it is to be a human being, when Tommy lunges. He jumps from the bank into the mud, grabs the bird as it attempts to launch itself away from danger, and, in an awkward twisting of limbs and feathers, falls backwards into the water. But he has the bird firmly against his chest, and when she realizes she's caught, she holds very still. I notice that she seems much bigger in Tommy's arms than when she stood alone on the bank.

I watch as if what's happening is not quite real. I'm in a sort of shock, I suppose. Tommy is in the mud, trying to stand up without losing his hold on the egret, and I'm wondering why the bird doesn't use her beak. She could hurt Tommy and be free if she did.

Tommy manages somehow to get to his feet, and he begins shouting to me. "Open the trunk. Gimme the keys." He's coming at me with the egret wrapped in his arms, staggering as she shifts her weight from one side to the other. He reaches one hand toward me, fully expecting my help.

"Let her go," I say.

"No. Just gimme the keys."

"Let her go, Tommy."

He walks up the short bank and right past me toward the car, figuring, I suppose, that I'll give into him as I always have before. What I do, though, is something different. I can't let him put the bird in my car, and I can't let him walk away with it, out onto the road. I know only two things for sure—I don't want to see the bird hurt and I don't want to see Tommy in jail.

I walk over toward the car, the keys in my hand, and offer

them to Tommy. He reaches out his left hand with difficulty, still fighting the bird with his right. I grab his wrist and use the only wrestling move I know, one I remember using as a kid, one I probably used on Tommy when we were ten. I twist his arm behind his back.

"Let go of the bird, Tommy."

"Please."

"Let it go."

"No. Don't ruin this for me. I want this."

I yank his arm until his hand is bent up over his opposite shoulder, and the white bird breaks free. It hits the ground, landing on its feet, then pushes up and flies quickly over the water. The bird cries out much louder than I ever imagined it could, and it keeps crying as it flies off toward the trees.

Then I look for Tommy. He's on the ground, crying too.

For the next ten minutes, he won't speak to me. I try to calm him down, and finally I succeed, but he won't come home with me. He eventually walks away and I drive home alone, only to sit awake all night, waiting for him, worrying that it was a mistake to let him leave.

IN THE morning I get a call. A psychiatric nurse tells me that Tommy has admitted himself to the hospital and has named me as the person to contact. I take over his clothes, but another nurse says Tommy doesn't want to see anyone. Two days later, he's sent to a state hospital, then eventually to a group home. He still lives there, in fact, and works as a carpenter, and writes to me and says he is happy.

I continue to visit the lake for a while, not every night, but often, and I continue to watch the birds. I think about Tommy and his vision and why he dragged me out there night after night. I'm not sure I understand, but eventually I take his advice and call Laura. After the third phone call, she agrees to come see me.

I take her to the lake. I tell her what occurred to me one night while I was watching this one white bird. It was a week after Tommy admitted himself, and I was watching this bird and wondering if it was the one Tommy had tried to capture. What occurred to me was that our baby is not dead, but is out there somewhere, still waiting to be born. Like a small bird, I say to Laura, a small bird hovering in the sky and looking for a place to land. I tell her I want us back together again. And she agrees.

So here we are, spending part of each evening walking slowly around the lake. We watch the birds a while, then we go back to the apartment and do what we can do, whatever it takes to guide our baby home.

Memento Mori: Premonitions
Shelley Puhak

1.
I felt you quicken on a cliff, flutter
while we clutched, queasy,

and the bus rushed up to a precipice,
swung around to stone wall, rattling

the whole way to Pompeii
and the plaster cast under museum glass:

a pregnant woman, her
curling, clutching shape in seaside ash.

2.
In the House of the Vettii,
the patron saint of Pompeii weighs
his penis in fresco: ochre,

carbonate of copper, vegetable dyes mixed
with soapy limestone, polished off with wax.
His monstrously red member
makes me nauseous, nervous.

And when your own penis, modestly sized,
digitized and ghostly gray, swerves
to the center of the ultrasound screen,
I go squint-eyed with tears.

3.
Sky—shifting indigo and slate,
incandescent with disaster, rain
of cinders on the cobblestones.

I tell them my dream—
a crying baby, rivulets of ash
streaking his cheeks—
but they call your heartbeat
a metronome.

Six weeks later, the curtains drawn,
the clocks stopped,
the mirrors draped. I sit vigil—
a rabbit, dilated
in the present participle,
dying. They paint your
tiny pale penis
with iodine; they watch as
the metronome crumples
into ash and bone scraps.

4.
I dreamt my stomach swung open like
a refrigerator and I plucked you
out—you, a doll, with unblinking obsidian

eyes, limbs unfurling mechanically.
They said to shelve you a while
longer, and I agreed, but first

I peeked between your legs
to make sure. And there it hung, tiny

and too-pink, a little tongue
that told me nothing.

Miscarriage
Elizabeth Schott

I am thinking now
about the one who chose—
and I do believe it chose
knowing everything beforehand—
to be just this bright spark,
the one who saw the brief
extent of the life ahead
and then still entered into it.
I am thinking about the one
who took on the agony of mitosis
without being able to expect
the triumph of a pulse,
the one who chose to ride down
in the boat that is of your body
and of your mother's body
and her mother's and so on
without being able to see—
already having seen—
your face.

I believe I am supposed
to use the word angel here,
but hesitate, finding it overused,
and yet now seeing that we
use it so often because
we are always grasping
after the kind of a one
who has, just now,
come and gone within you.

Shooting the Strays
Rose M. Smith

Today they are shooting the strays at Kangirsuk.
Angels of mercy hold hot deliverance with both hands
to cull the crop of canine indiscretions
in Inuit villages nestled in the North.

I am reminded of dilation and curettage,
saline solutions, partial-birth removal
of smaller, much more human problems
before nuisances can be born,
before they gather in groups at daylight,
roam in packs at dusk,
hustle up to hilltops, street corners late at night
to howl like some ancestor at the faintest moon.

To the North, the Inuit slowly yield to protest,
agree to neuter sources they think that they own,
shield their eyes from the culling,
avoid the faces of rifled men,
preferring they remain unknown.

Here we pass anonymous
protestors gathered near the angels' gates,
oblivious of gunfire ringing through arctic wilds,
of the yelp and hush of last breath, absence of breath,
the second screams of those who fail to die quickly,
the sharpening of knives to harvest what remains.

breathe
in

Listen
Lisa Alexander

*I*t begins with eggs (not that kind of eggs.) A roadside joint in Maui, me pushing around my scrambleds, Liam, head down, mechanically eating his huevos rancheros and sending a shiver of thirty-years-down-the-line into our romance. He swallows. I can trace it going down his throat. He wipes his mouth and says, "Before we decide to be together, I would want to have you tested to make sure you could have our child."

"What?" I sputter, and he looks at me in that petulant way.

"See, this is the reason I can't be with you. You're run by your emotions. You have no control."

Then I cave. I always cave. Caving is the story of my life, but this time is different because not all of me caves. *Fertility!* my body cries in a high drama voice only I can hear. *I'll show you Fertility!*

And—ha!—show us it does.

Picture a tin roofed hut on the wild side of Maui. The rain on the roof sounds like an AK-47 target practice because Hurricane Iniki is flattening the island of Kauai not far away. We are stupidly not afraid. Instead we are high. We have just decided to break up for good and, to make it especially hard, we've taken X, the love drug.

After a while, we wobble into the garden. The emerald lawn is spangled with jasmine and rimmed with towering palms. Across the one lane highway, the ocean is angry. The waves are not lapping, but chomping on the beach, sucking up chunks of crabgrass, spitting out shells and stones, slurping across the asphalt.

We shed our clothes like the useless skins of strange white fruit and run naked in the rain. A few miles away, Iniki lifts off the roof of a three bedroom house while we dress each other in flowers. I wedge a white hibiscus in Liam's black Irish curls. He works hard on a necklace of starry jasmine, stems growing brown in his hands. Before long, we switch to kissing, his hands mapping my breasts, his body on mine, flowers crushed and slipping, and then he's inside and, there it is, the moment I conceive.

TWO MONTHS pass and I know this immediately when I get the test from Sav-on, pee on the absorbent strip and watch, amazed, awed, and then scared as the liquid seeps first into Window Number One, then Window Number Two, making little purple bars in both.

I sit with it maybe sixty seconds—which is not a very long time—before I get on the phone. "I'm pregnant, but don't worry, I'll take care of it."

Fool.

"I'm pregnant but don't worry I'll take care of it."

Fool, fool, fool.

On the other end, I hear a pause. It terrifies me. I will do anything, say anything, be anything to fill up that pause, but then I've already done it, so I say nothing. After an endless wait, Liam finally comes up with, "Okay." Again, no words come from my mouth.

After the abortion is performed (performed?) by a gynecologist who is too handsome for that kind of a job, I can't pee for a month. My bladder quickly reaches the size of a balloon. I go back and he catheterizes me into a pan. Beaming his white teeth at me, the gynecologist says, "You worry too much."

Next I go to a nice young urologist who teaches me how to catheterize myself and suggests I learn to relax.

For a while, I carry the straw and K-Y in my purse. The jelly leaks through an invisible hole, puddling in the bottom of my bag where it collects mysterious sand and gummed up coins. I tell myself I don't feel anything, but this is a lie and my body knows it. It has lots to say and only one way to say it.

While Liam goes back to pick-up games in the park, ordering takeout, working on his book, shopping for girls, I can't go back to anything. I can think only of water. My body insists on my attention with jelly, straws, and a burning urethra until I finally get it: I am pissed off. Pissed off—get it?

Oh, clever body. Witty body. Subtle body. I will always listen to you from now on.

FIFTEEN YEARS later, the hot stream of my pee hits another pregnancy stick, fibrous as a piece of sugarcane. Wonder, awe, horror—all of it again. The wet spreading through the little windows with their splash guards, the twin purple bars going from blurry to clear. This time I carry the stick into my bedroom where my husband of ten years is lying, reading glasses low on his nose, peering at a *New Yorker* article about the mujadheen.

"You won't believe this," I say climbing on our bed. "I'm pregnant."

We both grin, hard not to. I'll be 45 in a week, and Miles has just hit 55. We have one daughter; she's been enough. I've assumed myself peri-menopausal, and now, and now, and now....

"B is for boy," I say, pleased with my psychic ability, "I'm sure of it."

"But it's nothing yet," Miles says. "A cell."

I look at him. He's got good, kind eyes, but I can see what's going on. I think, *Baby.* He thinks, *Money, where do I get the money?* I say, "Boy," he says, "Cell." And there it is again—the pause—and me, saying, "Don't worry, I'll take care of it." Immediately I can feel the fear ebb in Miles.

"You know I love babies," he says, and I hear this, I really do.

I give him a smile, "And you know I don't." I'm not one of these mothers, I think proudly, who needs to be needed by a bundle of joy. The indescribable sweetness of my relationship with our daughter has grown as she's grown up. I don't need more. And, at the same time, I realize with a flush, my body's been talking to me for the past two months, and I haven't heard at all.

Witness the migraine I call the Evil Flower. Sixty two days ago it showed up and moved in between my eyes. Shrieking stabs at the slightest noise. Strobe flashing lights. I keep thinking of the U.S. Navy hammering spikes into dolphin brains to prove they could feel. I go to everybody. Allergists. ENT guys. A neurologist who plays violin in the mall on his days off. I pop handfuls of meds with names like gods—Topamax, Zomig, Dyazide, Prednisone, Valium, Vicodin, Percoset, Lortab, Maxalt. I allow them to stick needles up my nose, cameras up my sinuses, to wheel me into a giant clicking CT tube while I think of death. They are excited about looking for tumors when I finally pee on the string, and hear what my body had been screaming all along.

THE DECISION—you heard it—assumes itself. I feel joy in my fertility, along with frustration, guilt, but no grief or loss. *What's wrong with me? Walled up. Choked off. Am I a house with the windows glued shut?* There is difficulty in getting a termination—that's what they coyly call it now—before a holiday weekend. Finally, I get on the schedule. My gynecologist will do nothing, however, without an ultrasound, and so I find myself in a waiting room. The doctor's gay and flouncy name is Rita. Dusty silk flowers spring out of a vase. Renoir's *Mother and Child* stare at me blandly through their watery blue eyes.

"Can you fill out these forms now? I need everything." The nurse at the front desk hands me a thick sheaf. My head still hurts. The nausea crouches in my throat. I don't want an ultrasound. I know it's a boy, and I don't want him to be a boy anymore; now I want him turned back into Miles' nameless, faceless cell.

Dr. Rita pokes her head out. "I can see you now."

We walk to the examining room where I put on a paper gown made of the same stuff as the tissue paper hearts that litter the ground after weddings. As I put my feet in the stirrups, Doctor Rita says, "Slide down. That's good."

She spreads the jelly on the probe, and swivels the monitor away. 'This is a termination so you don't want to see, right?'

The excuses fall out of my mouth, "Misdiagnosed... X-rays... I took all these drugs."

The light from the monitor reflects in Dr. Rita's glasses as she says, kindly, "Shhh, don't move." Then she is quiet, adjusting the probe, watching the screen.

"I'm pregnant, right?"

"About two months." Dr. Rita takes the probe out and swivels the monitor back.

"There's good news. You might want to look."

On the screen, a cone of white spreads against a black background. In the center is a shape, a peanut of light curled inward, slightly larger at one end. I flash on the ultrasound of my daughter, that same cone of staticky white, that sense of astronomy, and she, bigger than this, curled also in the center, thumb clearly wedged in mouth, but where Grace pulsed with life, this tiny shape is completely still.

"See—no discernible heartbeat; it's gone."

And I feel it then. A sharp contraction in the area that must be my heart. That magic spark, part Miles, part me, part something else, that spark that caught and grew, a system electrically throbbing and pulsing and, just as suddenly, stopped. And I realize something else too: I was proud of him, plucky little guy against the dry riverbed of my fertility, a possibility of a boy who survived... and now... and now... and now...

THE FIRST one was an abortion. The second one was my daughter. The third is an evacuation. My doctor says that recent law—I assume the tyranny of the religious right—has it that her clinic cannot administer pain medication to a woman aborting a child. She tells me to dope myself up before. It is not enough.

The doctor inserts a single strand of brown seaweed in my cervix, and I sit with it as the irritation of the salt and enzymes forces a gap eerily like a smile. Then, she fits a straw, and attaches a vacuum. The noise, loud and whirring, fills the room, my womb contracting rhythmically and sharply. For five minutes after, it pulses with labor pains before I am empty, cleaned out.

DAYS PASS. The nausea lifts, the headache recedes; my body goes hush. When I shut my eyes though, I can still see streams of progesterone and estrogen waning and waxing. I can see all kinds of things. I can see a life force like the sea in the eye of a hurricane surging across a green and spangled lawn.

I will listen to you, sweet body. I will listen to you from now on.

By the Window
Kathryn Kerr

Weak with bleeding,
I command myself not to think.
Just look at the birds. They oblige.
Juncos and a chipping sparrow
check the cracks of the sidewalk.
The cardinal couple come
for sunflower seed. The jay
returns, a bit nervous, so close
to the cat in the window.
He fidgets, then flies. Even
Mr. Flicker waddles around
spilled grain, scowling others away.

Geese have left the pond,
moved back into the field
to glean, leaving the heron
to gawk and pose along the ice-
edged bank. The shadow
of an unseen hawk sweeps the lawn.
A child we never saw, a shadow,
crossed over our lives, still.

Blip
Tamara Keurejian

*i*t starts with the growing suspicion that you could be pregnant. Never mind that your period is still quite a few days away. You've already had one baby and know your body, and can pick up on all the subtle changes of those early pregnancy weeks. You already know what is too soon for a home pregnancy test to confirm.

You buy the EPT kit on your way to work, on the very day your period is supposed to start. It feels like you read the instructions a thousand times. Finally, in the harsh overhead light of the ladies restroom, locked behind the last stall, you urinate on the plastic strip. The instructions say it could take at least three minutes for the result. But in a matter of seconds a purple dot reveals your fate.

A week later a blood test and sonogram make it official. With your legs in the stirrups and a cold plastic wand in your privates, a complete stranger takes you on a guided tour of your uterus. You see the tiny blip of a beating heart. Any ambivalent feelings you may have had disappear.

The doctor says you're five weeks along. "Go home and relax," she advises. "Everything is okay."

For ten weeks it appears to be a normal, healthy pregnancy. Tender breasts, expanding waistline, queasy stomach. But one night, as you're drifting off to sleep, a terrible premonition jolts you upright. An eerie certainty that you will never hold this baby or know what its tiny face will look like overcomes you. You try to dismiss it as pregnancy jitters. Remember how nervous you were with the first one? Look at how beautiful she turned out.

The spotting starts one morning as you're getting ready for work. Nothing heavy, no cramping, but blood can't be a good sign. Trying to remain calm, you call the doctor and are told spotting is common during the first trimester, no need to be alarmed. Stay off your feet. No sex. If it doesn't stop in 24 hours, call back.

The bleeding is heavier the next morning. The doctor will squeeze you in later that afternoon for another sonogram. Until then she tells you to stay flat on your back, with your feet elevated. You lay on the couch staring at the ceiling and start making deals with a god you're not even sure you believe in. It's embarrassing how fast you find religion. You call your mom who tries her best to offer reassurance. But you can hear it in her voice. Wasn't it just a couple of weeks ago she told you to take it easy, stop working so hard, that this could be your last chance for another baby?

The agonizing hours pass, and now you chatter aimlessly with another patient in the waiting room. Classical music plays softly on the office stereo. Finally, it's your turn to go back. You pee in the paper cup. *So far so good,* you think to yourself. When the nurse weighs you, the scale shows you've lost seven pounds even though you're fully dressed and wearing heavy boots.

During the pelvic exam the doctor says everything appears to be fine, that your cervix is closed, nice and tight. You keep telling yourself: *you're worrying for nothing, worrying for nothing, worrying for nothing.* But you don't believe it.

"So, you're having some spotting." The sonogram technician enters the room. "Let's see what's going on here."

You tell her you're prepared for the worst but are hoping for the best. As she turns on the ultrasound machine she says you don't have to look. You know you have to. The fuzzy gray image appears on the screen and right away you notice there is no small black blip. Your heart starts breaking. Still, you have to ask, "Is there a heartbeat?"

"No," says the technician, "I'm sorry."

"Missed abortion" is the medical terminology for the demise of your pregnancy. The fetus actually died about five days before the spotting started.

A D&C is scheduled. You check into the hospital for the outpatient procedure a couple of days later, painfully realizing it will take place in the labor and delivery ward. As you change into a hospital gown you're surprised by how fast your body has regained its former shape—like it's trying to quickly forget.

You wake up thinking they haven't done the procedure yet, but you're told it's all over and you've been sleeping for more than an hour. You're groggy, but laying on the gurney you notice a nurse labeling a small bottle. The specimen inside would have been your second child. Now it's just something that will be tested for chromosome abnormalities and then disposed of in a medical waste bin. You ask to see the bottle. You don't know what to expect to see, but it doesn't resemble a baby. You're not sure if you feel relieved.

Days pass. The physical recovery is faster than the emotional healing. It seems like no matter where you go pregnant women, or newborn babies, are everywhere.

The doctor calls to tell you the lab results. The fetus was male and had Down Syndrome. As you put down the phone, all you want to do is hold the baby whose name would have been Logan, and tell him, "I would have loved you anyway."

Feel Better
Lisa Marling

My son curls next to his twin sister, who has yet to open her eyes to the world. She looks warm and content next to her brother, both in the crook of my arm. My son begins to root for food. His tiny hand, with the barely-there nails, digs as I guide my nipple into his mouth. He instantly falls into a tugging rhythm and closes his eyes. My daughter begins to cry, softly at first, then with urgency. She is hungry. Her cry becomes a wail but I cannot feed her. Instead, she slips from my arms into a little pink boat and begins to float away from me. She clutches her brother and my nipple pops from his mouth as he is pulled away from me too. They are crying, and my engorged breasts ache and burn—

i awaken. I want to vomit. I want to scream. I want to hold my babies and snuggle them to my neck. I want—

A perky little Candy Striper knocks on my door and before I can answer she enters, carrying a breakfast tray. I tell her I am going to be sick. She looks unaffected and suggests that I push the call button for the nurse. She leaves. I untangle the tubing connected to the IV in my hand and attempt to pull myself up in the bed. My lower abdomen screams and I push the button on the self-medication pump. Mercifully, I lose consciousness. This time I do not dream.

I WAKE to the sound of the lunch cart. God has granted me a morning reprieve. A nursing student enters my room and chastises me for not eating breakfast. She throws open the drapes and suggests I might feel better after the catheter comes out. The cafeteria woman delivers my lunch tray, and I attempt to pull myself up in the bed. The student nurse watches. I stop struggling and point out to her that my IV has infiltrated. She seems annoyed that I recognize this, but offers to let my nurse know. I hit my pump and sleep.

> *My eldest son is two. I am in an old house looking for him. I can hear him singing but cannot find my way to him. I am lost and he is lost.*

IT IS mid-afternoon and there is a nurse in my room. He is in the bathroom making a racket. When he comes out I ask him to help me move up in the bed. He asks me how I feel, but does not wait for me to answer. He tells me he is going to remove the catheter and that he is certain I will feel better as soon as the catheter comes out. He throws back the blanket and pulls my knee toward him as he pushes the other knee away. He uses the syringe to remove the water from the balloon that anchors the catheter in my body. I take a breath as he pulls the tubing from my urethra. He never looks me in the face. He tells me he is certain I will feel better now.

I close my eyes.

THE EVENING nurse appears at my door. She tells me she is going to remove my medication pump and IV. I silently scream. She asks me how I am doing and then tells me that I will feel better after the medication pump and IV come out because I will be able to get up and move around and make my way to the bathroom without assistance.

Visitors come and say little. They stare. Some ask questions but do not seem to want to hear the answers. They tell me I will feel better as soon as the incision heals and I get to go home.

IN THE morning I awaken to the sound of babies crying. I pull myself from bed and softly run my finger along the staples that hold my abdomen closed. I feel like everything would fall apart if not for the staples. I walk to the door and notice little plastic carts on wheels, and realize I am on the maternity ward. I softly shut the door and shuffle to the bathroom and pee. I shuffle back to bed and pray for sleep.

A student nurse enters. She is cheery and talks too much. She discusses the weather and last night's high school game. She talks about her one-year-old, and then asks me if I have any children at home. I answer yes. She tells me that I will feel better when I get home to my children. She tells me this won't be as difficult or sad since I have children at home.

I want to crush her skull. I look around the room for something I can use to crush her skull. Instead, I pray.

I feel sick and need to vomit. I hold a pillow to my lower abdomen and begin to wretch. The student nurse hands me an emesis basin and I miss, covering her shoes with bile. I pray again.

I AM released in the afternoon. The doctor says I will start to feel better soon. I leave with a hospital bag containing a toothbrush, toothpaste, comb, the clothing I had on when I was rushed to the hospital for surgery, and a pamphlet about the stages of grief. I have a sanitary napkin between my legs, a prescription for Darvocet, and a scar.

I vomit three times on the way home and I hold the hospital bag in the crook of my arm.

Delusion
Virginia L. Ramus

The baby was born dead.
The mother marveled
at the face of peace,
fading warmth of silken head,
before gathering,
tucking the child
back into her womb
to be born again later,
properly.

Sharing the Weight of Memory
Ellen Shriner

i was washing the supper dishes, while my sons played in the kitchen, when my sister Margo called from Ohio.

"Hello…this is Margo…"

"Geez, I recognize your voice, for crying out loud." I was eager to hear if she'd had the baby. I'd returned to Minnesota from Ohio the day before, after spending the week helping Margo and her husband Pete prepare for their third child's arrival. Despite the miles, Margo and I remain close, talking weekly and visiting several times a year. Though I'm the oldest, she gives me as much advice and support regarding children and careers as I give her.

"Did you have the baby? How big is he?" I was impatient for the news, so I didn't register her "Margo Manager" voice. As the Assistant Director of a forty-person respiratory therapy department, she often dealt with personnel conflicts. When she was struggling to control her emotions with an employee, she made a point to speak slowly and clearly.

"Well…I have some news…he's not OK."

Electrified with fear, I struggled to focus.

"He's not expected to make it through the night."

"Oh my God, Margo. This can't be. What happened?"

"I went into labor after you left. Things were OK for a while, but then the baby was in distress. They did an emergency C-section. They got him out in twenty minutes—me scrubbed, them scrubbed, me knocked out. That's gotta be a record, but he had just inhaled too much meconium—poop. My best therapists worked on him, but there was just too much. It's sticky and thick and they just couldn't suction it out fast enough. His brain and major organs went without oxygen for too long."

"Oh Margo. I'll be there as soon as I can."

I FLEW back to Toledo in early morning darkness, and Dad was waiting for me at the gate. As usual, he wore his tan canvas jacket, but today, he looked smaller, drained, almost frail—a way I had rarely seen him. I saw the sadness in his bearing and the resolve I'd come to expect of him. Together we would do whatever was needed. I knew we'd eventually get through this.

We hugged and walked to the luggage carousel.

"The baby slipped away last night. It's a blessing, really. All his organs were shutting down – liver, kidneys, brain," he said with tears sliding down his cheeks.

My voice was husky, "It is a blessing. Waiting days for him to go would have just been harder." We both needed to think it was better, but nothing about the baby's death was right or good.

We drove in silence to my parents' house. There was nothing to say.

IT WAS only the first week of March, but all the snow had melted. The quick thaw left standing water on many of the flat Ohio fields. A light breeze rippled the surface of the water. Like my world, the natural world felt out of balance. Some force of reason and sense had slipped. I felt powerless to right it.

I hugged Mom and both our tears spilled over. Like me, she could imagine the pain of losing a baby, but she also grieved for her child going through this.

"Take my car—that way you can stay as long as you need. You'll…" Mom struggled to continue, "be a help to her."

She steadied her voice, "Call us and let us know how they're doing."

Outside her hospital room, I took a deep breath and braced myself. I had no idea what to expect. Would Margo be prostrate and weeping? Silent and closed in? Neither of us had encountered this level of loss before. I had no experience to guide me.

I heard her talking to somebody, explaining something. She sounded pretty normal.

"Margo?"

She sat on the bed talking to Pete's best friend Duffy, while Pete was on the phone. When she turned, I noticed her swollen, puffy eyelids. Her hair was pulled back into a messy slept-on braid and she wore two hospital gowns, one like a gown, one like a bathrobe.

She stood up gingerly, holding her incision, and we hugged.

"Oh Margo."

"I'm so glad you're here, but I feel bad you had to come back."

"I couldn't bear to stay away. I had to be here for me as much as for you."

"Did you ever hear that country western song that goes, 'There aren't enough tears in the world'? I just can't cry enough tears for this."

Pete hung up and we hugged. Grief had wound him up. He sat for a minute and then hopped up and began walking around the small private room.

"Margo, I think we should buy a plot big enough for all of us, so he won't have to be alone."

As he spoke, I recalled that Pete had experience with making funeral arrangements. When his younger brother died, he and his sister handled everything. His parents were too stricken to do it. Now he was making funeral arrangements again, for his own son. I thought, "This is so unfair. They wanted this baby so badly and now they have to bury him."

A priest knocked softly and stepped in.

"Is this a good time?"

Pete said, "He's going to do a blessing for Erik. They don't do last rites for babies." Though I had been raised Catholic, I was no longer devout enough to know the fine points.

The priest led us into a small oval room that was light and soothing. I steeled myself since I wasn't sure how bad Erik would look. For Pete and Margo's sake, I didn't want to show shock or revulsion, anything that would distance me from their child.

Erik lay on a gurney. Instead of a hospital gown, he wore a little blue and white suit and knit cap, which surprised but comforted me, because it made him look like the beloved baby he was. He was yellow from jaundice, and there were red marks where an IV had been placed in his scalp. But he looked like Margo and Pete's two girls had at birth.

I stepped closer to at least touch the baby. The others moved closer and we put our hands on his now-hard body, a benediction. I glanced at Margo and Pete supporting each other across from me, then I looked away, struggling not to sob. We cried silently. It felt important to maintain some control, that if I let go, we might all let go and fling ourselves over Erik's tiny body, wailing, the broken dam of grief pushing us under. My jaws and throat ached with holding back.

The priest said something meant to comfort, but I was out of the reach of his words. When he concluded, he led us away from that vortex of intense feeling. As we walked down the hall, the wave of heartache gradually subsided. I was relieved to reach the calm of Margo's room.

Duffy left and I settled Margo back in bed.

"How are the girls?" I asked.

"Lauren is really sad. I don't know if Katie gets it—she's only four," Margo said.

"They're taking turns playing in the baby swing," Pete said.

In spite of ourselves, we started laughing.

"You know how kids are—they'll figure out a way to have fun

no matter what," he said.

A few minutes later, Dad came to take Pete to the funeral home, so he wouldn't have to make the arrangements alone. I curled up on the end of Margo's bed.

"You know, I was under a general anesthetic when they delivered Erik, but I willed myself to come out of it enough to get a good look at him. I just had to know how he was. As soon as I saw him, I knew he wasn't gonna make it. So I slipped back under."

"Margo, that's amazing. I've never heard of anybody waking up from a general like that."

"I know. That's what my friend Luanne said, but I did. I told her what was happening in the O.R. right then and she said it was true."

She stayed quiet for moment then continued, "It's so weird. After all my years as a respiratory therapist, I have seen and done thousands of resuscitations and saved hundreds of babies. There are days when you have the best possible team and they still can't save the patient. Then another day, you've got the B team working on a patient with so many things wrong that the person doesn't stand a chance. That team's bumbling around and everything's going wrong, but still somehow that patient makes it. I had the A team. They could not have done things better or faster, but it just didn't matter."

WHEN I returned to Mom and Dad's, my older brothers were already there. Marty, the oldest, is single, never married. Despite the differences in their circumstances, he and Margo are close. He sat like a dark-haired bookend at one end of the sofa. Though all the Shriners are talkers—we normally go on at length about any subject of interest to us–grief made him mute. He listened while Dad talked out the afternoon's events.

Dave, the light-haired bookend, sat on the other end of the sofa. He and his wife Connie have three children: the older two are girls and the longed-for boy came third. He and Margo are comfortable together, but not close, yet Erik's death jolted him. He readily identified with Margo and Pete, and unlike Marty, he needed to talk.

"Geez. It's just such a shame. In this day and age, you just don't think of babies dying…maybe because it's always been so easy for us. I can't help but think, it could have been us. What if this had been Nick?" he said.

"I know. It's so unfair…and so random. Why them? Why not us? Why anybody?" I answered.

"When's the service?" Dave asked.

"Day after tomorrow," Dad said.

"Is it a funeral or just a service?" Dave asked.

"It's a service at the funeral home," Dad said.

"Why isn't it a funeral Mass? It seems like it ought to be a Mass," Mom called from the kitchen. She was unloading the dishwasher, out of sight, but not out of earshot.

I knew Mom wasn't trying to be argumentative. She wanted to pin down the facts. If she could just get the facts straight, then she'd know what happened. Then she could begin to understand and accept this tragedy. But now it seemed too large, too difficult to grasp and understand.

The next day I brought Margo home. Pete's sister Amy and her husband Bob arrived from Indiana and they were good for Pete. We got Margo settled on the sofa for a nap, and I went for a walk.

WHEN MARGO awoke, her milk had come in and her breasts were engorged and painful.

"Let me call the lactation specialist to see if there's something we can do," I offered.

I put down the phone, "The specialist says to try cabbage leaves. "You're supposed to put them …" I couldn't even get the words out before I was snorting with laughter, "in your brassiere."

"Cabbage leaves? Cabbage leaves? What good will cabbage leaves do?" Margo squawked.

"Apparently, they have some kind of plant estrogen or something."

"Oh for Christ's sake. Give me a break. Don't they have some medicine for this? It's not like it's going to hurt the baby."

"She said they don't give medication anymore. Nature takes care of it."

"That's it? These boobs are rock hard."

After the girls were in bed, Pete and Margo and I had a glass of wine. While I was putting the wine away, I grabbed the cabbage.

"How about those cabbage leaves, Marg?' I teased.

I rinsed a few and shook the water out of them.

Pete looked at them and said, "Those are too big."

It was funny to realize that I was as familiar with Margo's body as Pete was.

I cocked my eyebrow at Pete and said, "Not today they aren't."

"Give them here," Margo said.

"You aren't gonna do that in front of the kitchen window," Pete said.

"Sure I am."

She pulled up her shirt and tucked a cabbage leaf into each side of her brassiere.

"You know, that's not too bad. They're kinda cool on my skin. They might help."

Pete stood in front of the window and waved at the house behind theirs.

"Show's over, everybody. Stop by tomorrow, she'll be back," he hollered.

THE NEXT morning I handed Margo a mug of coffee.

"I hate to ask this, but what do you want to wear for the

service?"

"My bathrobe."

"Nobody will mind if you do."

"No. I need to do better than that for Erik. But can you pick out something?"

I pulled three dark maternity dresses from her closet, thinking, *I can't believe we're doing this.* She rubbed her hands over her large empty belly. She still looked as if she were five months pregnant.

"How about this paisley one?"

At the funeral home I hugged my brother Dave and his wife Connie.

"Christ. I can't believe this," Dave said, wiping his eyes.

"Here. Puffs. I'm going with the industrial strength kind now."

He and Connie smiled.

My parents stood by Margo and Pete. Tears slipped down Dad's cheeks constantly, and occasionally he brushed them away as he spoke to people. Mom steadily dabbed at her eyes with a tissue and didn't say much.

Pete led Lauren and Katie over to the small white casket. I had no desire to look at it, so I circulated through the mourners restlessly, introducing myself to Margo's coworkers. It felt bizarre, as if I was socializing at a wedding reception, but I wanted to acknowledge their concern. After speaking to everyone, I joined my brother Marty in the middle of a long row of white folding chairs

Music signaled the start of the service, the rest of the chairs filled quickly. The useless words washed over me, empty of comfort or wisdom. I didn't blame the priest. There was no explanation good enough. But as he said the final blessing, I was snagged by the familiar, serious prayer used only at funerals, "May perpetual light shine upon him." The service no longer felt surreal. The finality of the moment began to sink in.

I felt pulled back in time, hand-over-hand down a rope knotted with memories—my Grandma Mimmie's funeral, Grandma Pleitz's funeral, my grandfather's funeral when I was in third grade, my second grade classmate's funeral. Those griefs were small now in face of this one, but they all felt tied together, a lifeline I could use to pull myself through this sorrow.

AT THE gravesite the ground was springy and saturated. A fresh breeze carried the scent of spring—new leaves and damp soil. Margo, Pete, and the girls stood at the head of the casket. Mom and Dad and I stood next to them. The rest of the family completed the circle.

I trembled uncontrollably from nervous tension. Dad put his hand on my shoulder, steadying me, and I braced against the onslaught of emotion. The priest said his words in the singsong cadence of prayers that have been said too often and I drifted on the surface of them. But when he intoned, "Ashes to ashes, dust to dust," I was jerked under, immersed again in the reality of what we were doing. Hearing the words I'd heard at every funeral since I was a child completed the ritual and moored me to the desolation familiar to all bereaved families.

After the priest stopped speaking, Pete went down on one knee and put his hand on the casket, brokenhearted. The childhood image of a guardian angel kneeling with its arms spread out protectively flashed through my mind. The girls put their arms around Pete, and Margo put her hands on the girls' shoulders. Their raw suffering and the finality of burying Erik caused something to give way in me and I sobbed, swept under by their pain and loss. When the wave pulled back I was weak and weary. We turned from the gravesite and left.

THE DAY after the funeral, Margo's house looked like the morning after a party. Paper plates were shoved into an overfull garbage can. Half of a bakery cake sat on the table and leftovers from the funeral lunch filled the refrigerator. The kids, who needed a break from sadness, played Barbies and house, which mostly involved pushing Katie in the baby swing. Though the sight of her in the swing grated on us, we didn't have the heart to make them quit.

Amy washed dishes, but the rest of us were exhausted by the events of the previous days. Margo and I drank coffee as if that was all it would take to pull us out of our listlessness.

At the funeral home I'd noticed a distraught woman who had spent a long time talking to Margo.

"Who was that woman who was so upset at the service? Somebody from the hospital?" I asked.

"Sort of. There's a guy I know who works in maintenance. That was his wife. They had a stillborn baby ten years ago."

"Wow. That was nice of her to come to Erik's service when she doesn't know you that well."

"Well, I guess she really identifies with me," Margo said.

"Even ten years later, her feelings seem pretty strong."

Margo put down her mug, straightened her shoulders and looked me in the eye. "You know, I'm not going to be her in ten years," she said. "I'm not sure how I'm going to do it, but I'm going to move through this. I refuse to be stuck in the same place ten years from now. I've got two girls and a husband who need me."

I hugged her, saying, "I'm not sure how you're going to do it either, but I'll help you however I can."

For the first time in the last few bleak days, I felt hopeful. I had understood intellectually that our grief would eventually pass, but now I really believed it could.

THE PLANE made a large arc over northwest Ohio and turned toward Minnesota. I longed to see my husband and boys, to scoop them up and hold them tight. I knew I couldn't protect them from anything, but I could cherish them and be grateful for the gift of their presence. I remembered a week ago I'd crabbed at Greg for being messy and scolded Mike for being sassy. None of that was important. They were alive.

A MONTH later, all across Minnesota rivers flooded—the Mississippi, the Minnesota, and the Red River. Water rose silently inch-by-inch, creeping across the wetlands, stealing the flatlands where we thought people, not rivers, belonged. Nearby, it went up eight silent and relentless inches overnight. Familiar landmarks disappeared. I watched the water and felt grief's eddies pulling at me.

Weeks after the flooding subsided, I walked along the Mississippi River. The grass was tan and silty and still swirled from the water. Rubble that had been swept in the water's path lay strewn across the grass: branches, a red knit glove, plastic bags with puddles of brown smelly water, scraps of newspaper, bleached paper cups, and a gold hoop earring. Where was the kid that belonged to the glove? When did the earring get lost? How did all these things come to reside together? I couldn't make sense of the miscellaneous pieces brought together by circumstance.

I haven't made sense of the odd mosaic of feelings that remain after Erik's death either. Erik suffocating even though Margo is a respiratory therapist. Pete's incredible strength and focus when arranging to bury his son. The silliness of the cabbage leaves. The unexpected comfort of familiar prayers.

But now, I see grief as the force of nature it is. It swamped my family and tumbled us impersonally like sticks in a stretch of whitewater. We were caught up in its torrents, driven along helplessly, and set down in a new place.

I don't understand the why of death any better now. But the world no longer feels as if it's unbalanced, slipping off its axis into chaos. Since Erik's death, I better understand that I am connected to the timeless basics of human experience: birth and death, love and grief.

Birth Stories from a Warrior Goddess
Laurie Soha

each mother, through the course of her children's lives, gives them little platitudes as motherly gifts. They are those "words to live by"— ones that will echo in her children's heads throughout the rest of their lives, for better or worse. Some are noble sentiments like, "Be kind to your sister, you will need each other." Some are trite sayings such as, "Don't sweat the small stuff." And some are sayings left over from your own mother like, "Always wear clean underwear in case you're in an accident."

I give my girls these sayings to pack away carefully. I see them leaving home with a little knapsack on a stick, stocked with Mom's Words to Live By. But, along with these platitudes and whimsical thoughts, I send each one forth with the story of her birth.

Every mother tells her child of his or her arrival into this world. I have two daughters, and each of their stories is entangled with their siblings who never made it.

JOE AND I married when I was two weeks shy of my 30th birthday, and Joe was 36. I had been watching my biological clock tick over the last few years, so I felt relief, along with the joy of finding my husband. When I got pregnant unexpectedly in our first year of marriage, we didn't view it as an ill-timed, bad thing. I had wanted a little more time alone, but the years were piling up; it was time to begin the road to parenthood.

As the weeks progressed, my stomach remained fairly small— I wasn't attaining the curve of a pregnant woman. My OB had jovially asked me, "Where are you hiding that baby?" I just assumed I would blossom overnight into a rounder, more visible pregnant body.

DURING MY 21st week, I had a routine ultrasound. Joe and I were excited to actually see the baby.

The technician was initially quiet, then said she was concerned about the low amount of fluid around the baby. The doctor came in and looked at the screen. With a wary face, he recommended an amniocentesis.

I went to a perinatal group for the amniocentesis, and afterwards the genetic counselor told us to wait ten days for the results. She said *she* would call us; she didn't say she would contact my OB and have *her* break the news. So a few days later, when it came time for my next regular prenatal checkup, I went by myself not expecting to learn the test results.

Joe told me later that he was nearly in an accident on the way to the doctor's office. I know he regrets not being there for those initial dreadful words.

THE DIAGNOSIS was *triploidy.* Our baby had an entire extra set of chromosomes, and the physical anomalies were so great that she could not sustain life outside my womb. The low amount of amniotic fluid was an indication of my pregnancy's deterioration.

The OB tried to explain everything, and ushered us into a back lounge to watch a video. I was in such shock I couldn't register what was on that video—whether it was about genetic disorders, grief, or an infomercial.

Next, we ended up at the genetic counselor's office where the whole thing was explained to us again. We were given two options. We could continue the pregnancy until the baby died in utero, and then have labor induced. The doctors offered no specific length of time it might take for the baby to die inside me. Or, we could opt to induce labor right away, and thereby choose the day our baby would die.

I felt ill equipped to make the decision. *What was the best for the baby? What was best for us?*

That day we decided to induce labor. We went home with an appointment the next morning to check into the hospital and let our baby go.

Joe's brother, a pilot, was staying with us, as he often did between trips. It was his birthday, and Joe said we shouldn't ruin it with our grief. Later, I would think back and wonder why I didn't reply: "OK, I won't wail over my dying baby lest I rain unhappiness on your brother's birthday, even though he is a grown man and not a six-year-old!" Joe wasn't the only one to say or do odd things in the stressful weeks ahead of us.

EARLY THE next morning we checked into the hospital. Grief overwhelmed me, and I could not stop crying. We were sent to one floor where a friendly, open-faced man named Dr. Hamburger explained the procedure of inducing labor. His pleasant attitude was as jarring as his whimsical name.

Dr. Hamburger said I couldn't have an epidural on his floor, so if I wanted pain relief, I would have to move to the maternity ward—where I'd be within earshot of baby sounds. I had no idea what labor would be like, and I didn't want to regret saying no to pain relief, so I agreed to move to the maternity ward.

All night, nurses and doctors quickly slid in and out of my closed-door room trying to keep any baby's healthy cries from slipping through the cracks. Joe sat in a chair at my bedside, often crunching hard candy that sounded like gravel, and trying to lose himself in some novel the size of *Gone with the Wind*. Each time a doctor would enter, Joe would stand and hold my hand.

Perinatal doctors made fleeting appearances, but the residents managed most of the procedure. One resident, who I nicknamed Dr. Iron Hand, was rude and uncaring. Every thirty minutes, often without addressing me, he roughly shoved his iron hand inside me to check my dilation level. I was glad when his shift ended, even though he was replaced by a resident with deep, red bags under her eyes, who looked too exhausted to function well.

I did not feel the labor pains, but I suffered awful side effects from the medication—fever, vomiting, and complete loss of bowel control. Since the epidural anchored me to the hospital bed, I could not use the bathroom. No sooner did a nurse clean me, then the foul flood would overtake my body again. I apologized to one nurse who replied, "Don't worry, dear, I like taking care of you."

This compassionate nurse and others like her salvaged my dignity with their humanity and kindness.

Finally, a resident broke my water and I began to push. A football game flashed silently on the TV. The doctor with the blood shot eyes encouraged me. Joe and I asked when the baby would die, and if there was a chance she could take a breath. The doctor said the chances were zero.

I was never hooked to a baby heart monitor, so we didn't know exactly when our baby died. I just know that I had realized too late that I regretted being the one who caused her death.

When Lauren Mae finally slipped out of my womb, the nurses wrapped her deformed little body in a blanket and handed her to me. I held her in my arms, calmly called my mother, and listened silently as she cried. I felt nothing.

Then Joe took Lauren. Suddenly the most horrible-sounding sobs emanated from his body. He was sobbing the same way my father had cried years earlier after his son, my brother, died.

WHEN I was twenty, my brother Gary, and my cousin Todd were killed in a car accident. They were both only sons, and the only grandsons on my dad's side of the family.

Gary was seventeen. He was the kid everyone liked to be around—a comedian, actor, and the boy with a gorgeous baritone voice. Todd was only fourteen. He was an "All American Boy" with good looks, athletic talent, and a lot of promise.

In the initial days after the accident, family and friends took refuge at my parent's house, where everyone processed their grief in different ways. The house had two floors. The adults hovered downstairs. Their grief was raw and overpowering, and matched mine. In contrast, Gary's friends and my 14-year-old sister Julie stayed upstairs. They shared funny stories and happy memories.

I would often wander up and down the stairs, wondering where I should stay.

Occasionally my 17-year-old cousin Lisa, Todd's only sister, would join the young people upstairs. I noticed that she never cried. It was as if she was so overwhelmed by grief that her young psyche took refuge in not feeling. I could not identify with such numbness—until the moment when my first born came into the world.

MY PARENTS offered to bury Lauren next to my brother in Iowa. I went to a local funeral home, chose a little pink casket, and then boarded a plane headed to my childhood home. Joe didn't join me on this flight, but came later for the graveside service. He was a pilot too, and had access to the tarmac where Lauren's body was loaded onto the plane. He felt like he needed to be on the tarmac to urge the ramp agent to take good care of his baby daughter's body. He did that, because it was the only thing he could do for her.

My dad met me at the airport in Iowa. Together we picked up Lauren at the freight terminal where she was handed to me in a box. My dad carefully placed her in the trunk, and we went home to bury her by my brother.

When we had left the hospital, the nurse had assured us that we would have a chance to see our baby again at the funeral home. But in the small town where I grew up, the funeral director knew my dad. He told him that my baby had deteriorated so much that it was better if I didn't see her.

After my brother was killed, a different funeral director, yet another family friend, told my mother the same thing. He said Gary was so catastrophically injured, that it was better if she remembered him "how he was." My mother agreed, but has long regretted her decision.

I knew this, but I still decided not to open Lauren's casket and see her one last time.

THREE MONTHS after we buried Lauren, during the week of what would have been her full-term due date, I became pregnant again. This pregnancy progressed normally, and ended on a maternity ward too; this time with the door to my room wide open as I held my big, healthy, blonde baby girl, Michaela. There were no residents in sight.

In the story of Michaela's birth, she is the "One Who Was Meant To Be." I tell her that if her sister had lived, she would not have been born.

AFTER MICHAELA, I thought I had the birth process under control, and looked forward with optimism to having a sibling for her.

But my next two pregnancies ended in miscarriage. My OB sent me to a fertility doctor who offered to take me through an expensive process of injections and pills which may have slightly increased my chances for success.

Joe was worn out by the two losses in six months. I was running out of energy and hope too, but wanted a happy ending to the losses. One day Joe told his parents that he thought we should stop trying. My mother-in-law told him that I was very brave for wanting to try again.

I had wondered if I was just being foolishly hopeful, but being characterized as *brave* got my attention. I thought back to graduate school when a professor described the instant her children were born as "feeling like a warrior goddess, in control of her baby's birth and life." I began to think that maybe I *was* brave.

I decided to try again without the fertility doctor's process. I felt determined to be a warrior goddess, brave enough to continue the fight, even if I had to suffer more losses.

WHEN I was five weeks pregnant I didn't know if the pregnancy was viable. Alone in my room, I knelt down and prayed to the Virgin Mary to save my baby. I felt I had done the most important thing I could: I had appealed to the Queen of All Mothers to be my baby's advocate.

The next week, I returned to the fertility doctor's office for an ultrasound. On the screen we saw a heart beating like a Mexican jumping bean. I told the technician that at that very moment my husband Joe was in New York City, on his knees, praying in St. Patrick's Cathedral. The technician began to cry. In the car I shouted for joy.

Eight months later my second big, healthy, blond baby girl was born.

McKENNA'S BIRTH story is "How Mom Wouldn't Stop Until She Got You Out of Heaven." When I tell this story, I am the heroine.

I needed this triumphant end. Even after all these years, I still feel like a villain in Lauren's story. I wish we had spent a few more days pondering our decision to let her go. I wish we had consulted family, friends, and clergy. I wish I had done more to let my baby die in a more loving, peaceful way for all of us.

I also regret that I never opened Lauren's casket to see her one last time, hold her, and tell her how much I wanted her.

I can never erase what I didn't do for Lauren, but I often hope she realizes everything I did to get her sisters here.

I have a vision of meeting her for the first time in heaven. I imagine she is holding my brother Gary's hand and carrying a bouquet of wildflowers. Gary sees me first and waves elatedly, and then Lauren looks up at me with joyful recognition. She races to me and I throw her up in my arms, inhale her sweetness, and whisper to her all those wondrous moments of her sisters' childhoods that should have been hers too. I share these memories with her so that Lauren knows she was in my heart every moment of her sisters' lives, and because they are the only gifts I can give her.

A Reason To Be Gathered
Kerry Trautman

1.
The funeral wasn't like in the movies,
with wailing and rain.

2.
It seemed selfish to be sad
with all the April sun,
And it seemed selfish to eat so much
cake and cheese cubes afterward.

3.
I thought the white,
concrete coffin was...
bigger than a shoebox,
smaller than a snow-sled,
bigger than a high-chair tray,
smaller than a step-ladder,
bigger than a milk crate,
smaller than a toybox,
bigger than a case of beer,
smaller than a coffee-table...
I couldn't tell you dimensions,
if I tried.

4.
A couple brought their child—
four years old,
in a denim jumper with

ABC buttons.
The parents each
clung to one of her hands.
The girl tugged and squirmed.

5.
People brought flowers,
mostly pink,
        mostly in baskets,
        with pink ribbons and
        stuffed animals,
        stuffed bears, kittens, lambs,
        with pink ribbons,
        in baskets,
        with flowers,
        with roses and tulips,
        with pink and white
        carnations.

    6.
    The four-year-old girl
    couldn't understand
    why everyone was crying,
    with so many pretty flowers
    and stuffed bears and lambs.

      7.
      On our skin,
      the breeze
      with lake smell, was cool,
      but the sun was warm—

8.
The Mother didn't cry much,
because she already had
in nights before.
She didn't want the others
to stare at her with tilted heads and pity,
to use her for melodrama,
to use her to cry themselves.
Her eyes were drying-out
faster than her breasts.

9.
The Mother thought
how nice so many people came.
There was Uncle Barry
       who she hadn't seen since the fight
           about the dock space.
There was Cousin Sarah
       who didn't bring her two baby boys
There was Aunt Kathy from Toledo
       who was, maybe, crying
           for the first time.
There was little brother, Cody,
       who didn't understand
           how babies were born
           to begin with.
There was Aunt Ginny from Bowling Green
       who didn't understand
           why they needed
           a service at all.
There was Aunt Theresa
       who didn't understand why
           no one brought Kleenex to share.

There was the funeral home representative,
       who wore a yellow, satin jacket
               with his name and logo embroidered.

10.
I felt something like
       God was near,
something that knew
       the why of death,
       the why of giving flowers for death,
       the why of babies,
something that knew
       there was a reason to be gathered,
something that knew
       the reason,
       but wouldn't tell.

   11.
We stood,
       shifting in our dress shoes
               in a soft cemetery lawn
                       full of dandelions
                               that would be
                                       mown soon.

breathe
out

Thanksgiving Day, 2005
Anne C. Barnhill

At noon, the family gathered around a silent table
Where your two empty chairs waited.
We could not utter our usual litany of thanks for all
the world holds—

    The shaft of light coming through the stained
    glass in my office window,
    Early morning birdsong and late night walks
    across moonless paths,
    Our grandchild, your daughter, a four-year-old
    light in our sky—

All I could think of was you, how earlier, quiet and terrified
in the pink dawn,
you rode in the back seat with my son, his hand in
yours, his eyes holding you.
I couldn't remember the route to the hospital, blamed
myself for delays
Though the minutes lost would not have saved the
little one.

You didn't speak a word as your body oozed life,
your thighs sticky with it.
One quiet stream of tears slid down your cheek
as I steered into the hospital parking lot.
I saw my son take the back of his two fingers and wipe
your face.
I saw his furrowed, helpless brow in the rearview
mirror.

Many times, I've known such impotence—

> My own body, foreign, heaving my sons into the
> light—
> Our cat, bloody on the asphalt in front of our
> house—
> Unwarranted cells blooming into tumors—

A half-century has schooled me merely to trace
the erratic trajectory of cause and effect.

Clichés Don't Comfort Grandmother
Nina Bennett

God needed another angel.
What if I don't believe in angels—
what if I don't believe in God?

They're young, they'll have another baby.
They wanted this baby,
and they know you can't
replace one child with another.

Time heals everything.
How much time?
Weeks?
Months?
Years?
Eternity...

It's not like you knew her.
I knew my hopes for her,
I knew my dreams for her—
I've lost part of my future too.

She's in a better place.
I ask you:
Where is a better place for a baby
than in her mother's arms?

Fires Bear Down on Towns, October 30, 2003
Debbi Brody

There is nothing left of you.
In the Angeles National Forest,
the tree planted in 1986 to remember
burned in the wildfires of 1992.
Today, your ashes and bits of bone
were hurled in the flames
of California's largest wildfire.
The conflagration, like my grief,
stretches from Ventura County
into Mexico.

Twenty dead from the fire this week.
I weave your old-baby ashes
with theirs. If you were still
here, you would be leaving me
next year. Can this fire breathe
crimson on a night when sun
spot auroras fill the sky?
Is this the final burning, the one
that wrestles you to good-bye?

All I Know
Sarah M. Brownsberger

As I talk to you in the morning light,
my arms grow cold.
As I talk to you in the backyard dusk,
my knees buckle.
When you were lost in the earth
in your christening clothes,
were you desolate?

Your father says you are playing
with wooden spools and shells
as the old people knit and converse
in light from windows on the bay.
Such a beautiful child,
they might have exclaimed.
I thrilled, too, at the sight of you;
I love you more than earth can bear.

That Siren, Sleep
Jennifer Campbell

Startled by a cutting plea
from a cat she cannot see,
her heartbeat catches and climbs.
Again the disembodied mew
jerks apart the loose knot of sleep.

Each late night cry echoes
in the walls of her unnecessary womb—
a litany of upset stomachs, monsters
under the bed, pinching loneliness.

Hatred fingers its way through
her chest for the husband who
breathes ever more resolutely
with every cry. Yogic exhalations

cannot quite steel her against the thoughts
that will come. Tricks of the night
turn cat paws into human footfalls, release
noises from the barren nursery, rub out
the wrinkles, slippery lines of loss.

Soon sleep will wrap its tentacles
around her mind again. When slats of light
begin to shine through her closed eyelids,
she will find the other side of the bed
empty, her wrinkles returned.

Letter to My Daughter
Lois Lake Church

Spring 1984

My Dearest Emily,

In my sorrow over your death I search for understanding. I wait for a brilliant revelation to arise, phoenix-like, from the ashes of my grief. But I am not blinded by any flashes of insight. Rather, acceptance comes, gently and inexorably as the waves lap at the sand, as I ponder the lessons I learn from losing you.

I contemplate the concept of slowing down. I need to slough off the extraneous and take time to look deeply into things, seeing both for myself and for you. I have looked at this spring with new eyes, and have seen the rich purple-blue of an iris, flecked with yellow, convoluted; I have seen the goldfinch flashing its bumblebee colors in the sunshine, and they are wonders.

When I take time to "center down," I remember the joy of watching your movements roll across my belly like wind over a wheat field. Holding that joy in my heart, I try more often to look past your brothers' breakfast-time bickering or school-time stubbornness, to see shining sea-blue eyes, tender peach-curved cheeks, and hungry, creative curiosity.

Another Emily, a young woman in *Our Town*, Thornton Wilder's enduring play, has a chance to return to her childhood for a day, after she has died. Burdened by the insights she has gained in death, she is appalled to see her parents rush through their lives. Her words remind me to take time, slow down and look with delight at the details of my life "every, every day."

I ponder the idea of letting go, for all of mothering is a gradual releasing. When I hugged your brothers, I left my arms loose enough for each one to wiggle out of my embrace. I held his hand, learning to leave my fingers sufficiently open for him to be free to walk on his own, when he was ready. The infant becomes toddler, the toddler turns child, the child young adult, and each step needs me to loose the love-bond a fraction more.

But our goodbyes, precious girl, were so sudden, I had no time to learn you before you left me. One day I was filled with joy, with lively, stretching Emily; the next, with sorrow and emptiness. That one painful moment contained both our hello and our farewell. And now I must learn to let go of my grief.

Since you have died, Emily, I see how fragile and miraculous each child's life is. When I think of the miracle, I can more often breathe deeply and say something gentle instead of something sharp, smile over a spill, offer a hug rather than a spank.

And still, anger sometimes overtakes my intentions, because we are human. We are all different from each other. We are alive, with all the complications living implies. But now I see it is essential that we try not to say goodnight or goodbye when we are estranged, but rather to touch each other in love and acceptance

My months with you have changed me, Emily. For your sake I hope I can learn better to slow down, to let go, to make up. The joy I know, because you are a part of me, reminds me to honor you by the way I choose to live the rest of my life.

With love and gratitude,

Mama

Four Chambers for Tyler David Tandeski
Danielle Crawford

I.

It stinks like cotton swabs
turned cold
beside Mother's under-ripe belly.
Six months have passed.
She sits, waits: hunched, hurt
on that inhospitable bed.
I can't tell her this, but
she's aged a decade in a day.
Never looked so frail:
a daisy, withered by the worst of winters.

The October sky—
Mom's crying again,
laying above peppered linoleum,
under so many lights there's nowhere left to hide.
She's naked,
barren beneath the gown.
I try to resist, but join her, weep.

The doctor's eyes are dull with mock concern.
I, twelve, confused, want to escape.

In their crisply clean uniforms—
uniform sterility—
they stare, then speak:

The human heart has four chambers...

How were we to know God gave you only two?

Years of wait and worry plagued my parents.
Mom's stiff as the starchy parchment paper
she's now lying on.
Emotions repressed,
her words are strangled: *It's done.*

II.

Did we make the right choice?
After the initial miracle of you, I guess
we believed in invincibility.

An age-old wish, the desire to rewind.
Would it have been selfish—?

We thought of the steps
you never took.
We kissed the ground you never
set foot upon.
Since you've been gone,
we've lost our footing,
our solid ground.

I try to picture
what you'd be like now.
I've dressed your name up in costumes,
cloaked your memory with denial, anguish, rage...
anything I could muster, paralyzed.
I don't wish to remember you this way.
I'm back where I began:
without a clue.

The cotton, the clothing, that cold room,
my memory, too—
it's all too white.
I can't help but wonder if, taken,
you took color from our lives.

'99. Now seven more.
You would be eight, Tyler, had you survived
half a heart and Down Syndrome.
I'm greedy; I want you next to me.
You still are my brother.

I think of you,
whose footprint—only an inch!—
left a lasting imprint.

The human heart has four chambers...

Your heart was stronger than mine
for letting you go. We need

your malformed heart
to mend our own.

Expectancies
Shanna Germain

There is something she carries inside her all winter:
a curl of fist, a vestige of tail, lungs sucking liquid breath.
She carries it against the striking rain, against the hope
planted in her husband's face. She carries it against
her doctor's warning: there is a small risk.
Miscalculated into nothing, she lets herself believe
carries her hands across her belly like a woven basket
of her own design. She imagines come spring
she will open like a flower, let out nectar
for honey and the reflection of rivers after the rains.
New year, silence and sound
loss surging from her body like the flush
of stream emptying to ocean. Her hands
harden into clasps, into rope, the net of her
expectations caught tight against her skin.
First February rain, her husband glides against her,
ready to return to her shiny depths and try again.
In her mind, she walks along the river, watching
the slivers of silver—tiny heads, tails, eyeballs—
flashing again and again against the dam.

End of Memory
Jean Hollander

What can I bring you
after ten long years?
If you had lived
you would have been
too old for tears.
I pluck a sprig of purple flowering
that dried all winter and I set
it broken in the crust of snow
where deer have left
embroidery of hooves
around your stone.
From horror that remains
I raise you tall as I
your otherness, blue eyes, blond hair,
against my dark, having forgotten all
the details of your face except
your head against my neck
and that my last consoling was
to wash your things as though
you still could wear them.

Silence
Lisa B. Samalonis

My son Samuel, born early one September morning, never sucked in one breath of air or let out one cry of hunger or discomfort. I never got a chance to touch his flushed newborn face or look deep into his eyes like I did with my first two sons.

Instead, I held him silent and still.

That day all of my family's plans and dreams for Samuel died too. Yet, those dreams have not faded easily. My sons, William and Zachary, were just seven and five when I was expecting. They kissed and spoke loving words to my pregnant belly. They giggled, prayed, and made plans with their little brother—Christmas, bike rides around the neighborhood, playing in the park, swimming in the surf—plans that will never be lived.

In the first days after I came home from the hospital with no baby in my arms, many neighbors averted their eyes and hurried into their houses. Even good friends wouldn't talk about what happened. Some people advised me to pack up my grief, as though I could put it in a brown cardboard box and place it in the attic of my mind. They said, "Let go. Move on. Get over it. Everything happens for a reason."

I try not to judge or be angry with them. They do not understand this heartbreak; it's never happened to them.

My boys understand, but I worry that they have had to carry too much weight of loss and disappointment at such a tender age. Even as an adult, it is hard to grapple with the staggering sadness of Sam's death, and the hole in our lives it has left.

Once, Zachary was asked to draw a family tree for school. He left off a branch.

"Is there anything you want to add?" I asked.

"No." He paused and looked to me, "Is it okay?"

"It's a very nice tree," I said.

In writing Sam's name on his family tree, Zachary might have to explain what happened to his baby brother to his teacher—or worse to the whole class. He was not ready to do this.

I understood.

William speaks freely about Sam and his feelings.

One summer day, a year after Sam had gone, we played on the beach with friends and their nine month-old twins. The babies, dressed in fanciful white bonnets and pink swim suits, crawled through the sand.

William turned to me, with anguish in his eyes, and said, "I think of Samuel every time I see a baby."

I leaned and hugged him, pressing my face against his warm cheek. I whispered, "Me, too."

Another time, when I was napping on the couch, William nudged me awake. I blinked and saw his tiny face and startling blue eyes inches from mine.

"Good thing you didn't die when Samuel did," he said.

I sucked in my breath. "Good thing," I answered. "I asked God to let me be okay so I could take care of you and your brother."

A second later, he rushed off to play, but I was left wondering: *How many five-year-olds contemplate the death of their mother and their baby brother?*

Psychologists, doctors, and grief counselors all tell me that as long as the boys know that their feelings are heard, they will learn to deal with the loss and accept it. They will be fine, they say. I pray they are right.

A friend tells me that she believes my boys will grow up with a unique understanding of the fragility of life, and that they will appreciate things far more than other children their age. I hope she is right.

We honor Sam by talking about him—it keeps him alive. We know that silence, or pretending Sam's death did not happen, is not right. It happened. Talking about it is healing. It is acknowledgement and acceptance. "Sam lives in our hearts," the boys often say. Sometimes, they place a hand over their beating heart as they say it.

My children are healing me just as I am healing them, one conversation at a time.

Baby Blues
Christine Shaffer

i no longer attend baby showers, not even for family members or close friends. I don't like shopping for baby gifts, and I never buy one unless a baby is born.

I haven't always been this way. I used to enjoy picking out the perfect shower gift; I could spend an afternoon doing it. Now it only takes a few minutes before all those pastel onesies, terry cloth stuffed animals, and socks with lambs at Baby Gap make me almost lose my breath.

Last month, a pregnant acquaintance showed me her baby's ultrasound picture. "Look!" she said excitedly, shoving it towards me, "there's his head...his arms...his legs!" I forced myself to peek at it only long enough to see a blur of grey then pushed it back.

"That's nice," I said, feeling my throat constrict. At an earlier point in my life I would have cooed along with her, but I don't do that any more.

In fact, whenever someone tells me she is pregnant I cringe; I can actually feel my shoulders round. My eyes narrow. I get a close-fisted tightness in my stomach and then a wave of dread comes over me. I smile through it though, congratulate the pregnant woman, and quickly walk away. I've been this way for the past eleven years.

ELEVEN YEARS ago I was surprised to learn that I was pregnant two days before my husband and I were to leave for France. I had gone to the doctor complaining of vague stomach pains and nausea. "Should we do a pregnancy test?" the doctor had asked.

"Okay," I replied, shrugging my shoulders. The doctor called me later that day to tell me that I was indeed eight weeks along. This was my first pregnancy. My husband and I laughed. We swung each other around in an impromptu square dance.

In France we visited my relatives and told them we were expecting. We all toasted with champagne. One uncle showed me his private champagne stash. "When your baby is born," he said, pointing to bottles in the back of his cupboard, "We'll drink this—the real good stuff."

I ate steak and ice cream all week. My husband and I giggled constantly. We secretly decided to name our baby "Paris."

AT FIVE months I could feel my baby's quivering as though I had a big butterfly inside of me. I was excited and giddy. I loved that I was finally going to become a member of the club of mothers at my office who decorated their cubicles with framed pictures that said things like "A Star is Born," "First Birthday," and "Sweet Pea." I would soon have those frames in my cubicle too. I couldn't wait.

I adored the pregnancy world, especially the maternity shops where the sales people would offer me water and crackers, and bring clothes to the fitting room for me. These fitting rooms were gigantic and always contained a strap-on pillow so I could see how the clothes would fit as my belly expanded.

I enjoyed the baby stores just as much. My husband and I would walk through the aisles on Saturday afternoons looking at everything from outlet protectors to state of the art Italian strollers, feeling like we should buy everything immediately.

I liked saying I was tired, and how everyone would automatically understand. I enjoyed the deep, delicious, warm, and dreamy afternoon naps, especially on rainy days. I loved my first big, cushy maternity bra. I loved rubbing my stomach at night wondering if my baby's hand ever reached up to mine at the same time.

I was amazed at my growing body, slowly stretching itself. I watched documentaries on the beginnings of life, realizing it was now all happening under my skin, between my organs, cells feverishly separating, creating a human heart, a brain, a mouth.

Ordinarily I was cynical, but pregnancy was like a magnifying glass amplifying my happiness.

Until my five-month checkup. The doctor told me my baby might have spina bifida and scheduled an ultrasound. I had never heard those words before: spina bifida. I had purposely not read the chapter, "When Things Go Wrong" in the book *What to Expect When You're Expecting*.

The doctor looked at me after she had finished the ultrasound and said, "There are many things wrong with this baby, but for starters we're not getting a heartbeat."

At first I thought, *That's okay; they'll get it tomorrow.* But then I understood and began to cry. My husband, who had been holding my hand the whole time, dropped it and said, "Oh no."

The doctor turned off the ultrasound machine and explained that our baby had severe spina bifida, along with cystic kidneys, misaligned hipbones, and a malformation of the cerebellum.

It's all over, I thought as the doctor helped me off the examining table. *Just like that.*

THE NEXT day the doctor induced labor and my dead baby slipped out. The doctor wrapped the baby in a white blanket, put a small light-blue knitted hat on his head, and gave the bundle to me. I held my son's four-ounce, five-inch body as though he were alive. I could not bear to look at his face so I concentrated instead on his grey and wrinkled feet and hands which had light imprints of fingernails.

My husband also looked, but kept his arms at his side. A nurse wheeled in a bassinet, took my baby from me, and put him in it. I could see a blue card on the side of the bassinet with a smiley face that said, "I'm a Boy!"

"I'm very sorry," the nurse told me as she wheeled my baby out.

The same nurse returned a few hours later and gave me the tiny knitted hat with some spots of dried blood on the inside, and the blue card from the bassinet onto which she had inked my baby's foot prints.

My husband and I left the hospital that night with my overnight bag and a baby ghost hovering over us. I was afraid to let go of the pain, because I thought the memory of my baby boy would disappear.

People tried to comfort me in the following months. They'd say things like, "It was for the best," or "It was God's will." I hated it when they said those things. *Had God really singled me out for tragedy?*

TWO YEARS later I was pregnant again. This time, I avoided conversations about the baby. I didn't want any attention. I wanted to stay under the radar of the forces that decide which pregnancies will succeed and which won't. Sometimes people would wish me good luck. "Yeah, thanks," I'd mumble back and walk away quickly.

I waited until the sixth month to buy maternity clothes. I avoided baby stores and bought nothing—no crib, no clothes, no diapers. I thought it would be presumptuous to behave as though this pregnancy would produce a healthy baby, or a baby at all. If I could have had my way, I would have sat alone in a dark room for the entire nine months, kept my hands on my expanding stomach, and not moved a muscle to avoid upsetting anything.

Finally, when my daughter, Caroline, was born she was set next to me. I was so anesthetized the only part of me I could move was my head. The nurses wrapped Caroline in a blanket papoose and set her by my face where I was able to rub my forehead against her's. She was real. My daughter was alive and well.

WHEN PEOPLE ask, "Do you have just one?" it's too difficult to answer that I actually have two children. I don't tell them that I keep my baby boy's ashes in my night stand drawer, and that his ghost still haunts me after eleven years, forcing me to avoid pregnant women and baby showers. Instead, it's easier to say, "Yes, I have just one."

A Gift
Lynne Shapiro

i was recently asked, "So when did you decide to have children?" The question rubbed up against a subject that I'd finally become comfortable talking about, my multiple miscarriages. It took me years to get to the point where I could share my experiences; this only happened when I learned how to mourn.

MY HUSBAND Aaron and I didn't "decide" to have children. Soon after we met, I got pregnant. Deliriously happy, we gathered each other's families and set a wedding date. But before the end of my first trimester, I miscarried.

The afternoon I miscarried, Aaron and I were at his cabin on the lake. It was fall, and there was a profound stillness to the water, air, and me. I held onto my belly, the insides of which felt like Jell-O that hadn't jelled. My breast discomfort and fullness were gone. My hunger had disappeared. I felt no fatigue. It was as though someone flipped a switch from "alive" to "dead."

Aaron and I shaped "the baby that wasn't" into an "angel" credited with leading us to our commitment to a future together. Despite the miscarriage, we agreed to marry anyway.

FOR THE next seven years I got pregnant easily, but had miscarriage after miscarriage.

During these years it seemed like I lived in the "City of Women" all with babies. When women who were three or four weeks pregnant would announce their news I wanted to scream: "Too soon! Don't tell! Things go wrong!"

Dreaded baby shower invitations kept coming. The clapping, the unwrapping of pink and blue blankets, and the giggles that accompanied boxes of baby wipes made me feel like Typhoid Mary amongst the beatific. I quit going to them.

FINALLY, after seven years and multiple miscarriages, one pregnancy finally made it to term. During this pregnancy, I took Lamaze class with my good friend, Mary. One day Mary called my office to invite me to her baby shower. I instinctively said no, and offered the excuse that my mother would be in town. Mary said to bring her, and my husband too. She said there would be lots of people, both men and women of all different ages. The idea of my mother and husband bolstering me was appealing, so I acquiesced.

When I hung up the phone, I grabbed my purse, and headed for one of the great wonders of the Upper East Side, the second floor of Zitomer's Drug Store, a mini department store for the affluent. I picked out an elegant white knit baby outfit—hat, booties, and a onesie. The saleswoman placed each item in a separate box, wrapped them, and tied the boxes together with a perfect yellow bow. I left Zitomer's with a feeling of accomplishment.

I returned to my office and tried to work, but I was distracted by the Zitomer's bag. I couldn't resist opening the little booties. I was careful not to tear the paper so I could rewrap it according to the folds. I opened the box and took out the booties. I slid my fingers into them. It felt awkward touching the clothes meant for someone else so I quickly took them off and rewrapped them.

I tried to work again, but couldn't focus. I opened up the box with the little cap inside. I made a fist and put the cap on it. I cradled the cap, and rocked it. I had never held a bootie or a cap even one time during this pregnancy. Though I'm not a religious woman, I had unthinkingly followed the Jewish custom that calls for silence prior to a child's birth—no broadcasting one's business or hopes, and no gifts for an unborn baby.

But holding these baby items made me realize that I had treated the babies I'd lost as abstractions; I needed something concrete like the cap and bootie in order to feel their real absence—I had no sweet little head to fill the cap, and no delicious toes to fill the socks.

For the first time, I let loose and cried over my losses.

THAT WEEKEND I went to Mary's shower and handed her the gift. But I've held on to the healing the gift had given me.

The Lost One
Jane St. Clair

*i*t was 1978, a cold wet summer in the Appalachian hills of Kentucky. Bob and I had been married for almost ten years without children. I wanted a baby so badly that my obsession was ruining my marriage, my career, and my life.

My gynecologist had an Alice-in-Wonderland view of pregnancy. Take these pink pills for ten days to grow a fat uterus. Have sex on days eight through ten as often as you can. Take these blue pills on days ten to twenty-eight and, abracadabra, you will make a baby.

But nothing came of it. Each new flow of menstrual blood was another defeat: a red badge of failure. I got such bad headaches from the blue pills that I could no longer concentrate at work. Nevertheless, Dr. Wonderland upped his ante. Take two pinks per day. Take three. Take four. Take six blues. When I grew discouraged, he told me, "Rome was not built in a day."

I felt so envious of pregnant women that I could not go to baby showers and celebrate their happiness. I felt like running over strollers. When another friend or relative got pregnant, I became depressed again.

Older women told me to relax. One particularly cruel one advised me to "Just eat apple seeds." Everyone told my husband and me to take a long vacation. A year past, and then another.

I finally joined a support group, a local chapter of "Resolve." Meeting and commiserating with other infertile couples only made me more depressed. Their obsessions mirrored my own.

One woman in our group had undergone fifty-three artificial in-seminations. Others had a variety of surgeries to open up their tubes and remove cysts or other obstructions. Many couples had been trying for over a decade. The motto of the group was "Never give up."

When I quit, our leader was nice and said "Resolve is all about resolving the issue. You resolved it your way." Indeed, I had. I told Bob that the child we both wanted so badly was not meant to be. That was that. I stopped seeing Dr. Wonderland, I stopped the support meetings, and I took a job that kept me away from home. We talked about adoption.

When I skipped a period, I did not think it was important. My hormones and periods were so messed up from all the fertil-ity drugs I had taken that I often skipped periods. However, my breasts were swollen. I felt very tired and weak.

I put off seeing a doctor because I convinced myself I had a dis-ease from the carcinogens Dr. Wonderland had dispensed to me. After all, I had signed a million waivers to the effect that someday I could develop ovarian, breast, or liver cancer. It was the deal I willingly accepted to get a baby.

After I missed three periods, I finally saw a fancy doctor. He confirmed that I was about four months pregnant.

My husband and I felt joy. We pictured our own little one, and couldn't wait to be a family of three. We even worried about our dog's feelings after we saw *Lady and the Tramp*. We dared to paint a nursery and buy little toys. We named our baby Eric Christian.

One day there was brown blood on my tissue. I called my doc-tor who said to wait a while. I felt entirely lost, and I walked around the golden woods by myself. It was September, and the leaves were the color of antique paper, the color of decay, the color of endings not beginnings.

I went to the fancy doctor. He prescribed bed rest with my feet up. He said to wait another week. I tried not to use the bathroom, because every time I did, there it was again. I could not read or concentrate.

I went back to the doctor. He told me in a very matter-of-fact way, "The fetus is dead. There's no heartbeat."

I could not control myself. I ran out of his office into the waiting room. I told Bob to take care of things. He arranged appointments and scheduled the minor surgery that would take our baby away forever. I sat in the car and cried.

It rained with snow flurries on the day of the D and C surgery, and there was a winter chill in the air.

The doctor scraped my womb clean of any trace of the baby. He came in my room and told me the baby had been terribly deformed and that this was a blessing in disguise. I recalled how he told me so bluntly that my baby had died, and now he was bluntly telling me that my baby was deformed. He may have been a doctor with the highest credentials, but he was failing me as a human being.

I did not care if my baby was deformed: I loved him anyway. I pictured my deformed baby roaming around heaven without his mom or dad. Lost.

A FEW months later I was walking up a flight of stairs to my office, when suddenly an image of my dead grandmother came to me. She was holding Eric Christian in her arms. They looked as beautiful and holy as the *Madonna and Child*. I finally felt that my little lost boy had been found.

Cutting Glass
Kathy Schofield Zdeb

Cutting glass is a daring act, all slivers and sharp edges. Consider this, from an instruction manual on stained glass: "The main obstacle when snapping glass by hand is imagining yourself with gashed fingers." Painful, indeed.

My temperament is more suited to fabric arts, where forgoing a thimble constitutes bravery. Embroidery, quilting and batik once engaged me; all taught me that craft is as much about process as product.

Grief is also a process. Stained glass shed light on mine, the full spectrum.

Ten weeks into my second pregnancy, blood blossomed. Spotting accelerated to hemorrhaging, then a D&C. I returned home empty.

How to explain to my four-year old? I told Sara that sometimes when gardens are planted, even though the bulbs are placed with care and nurtured, not all of them will blossom. They are flowers that might have been.

Eight months later, I repeated the metaphor.

A microorganism was the suspected cause of the miscarriages. Scientists later would discover that the species has one of the smallest genomes known to sustain independent life: 470 genes. What kind of evolutionary insult allows a mere speck to abort babies that might have been? Who would have run and jumped and laughed and cried? Who would have felt my touch, known my love?

The doctor prescribed tetracycline; I self-medicated with stained glass.

Each morning after leaving Sara at preschool, I carried my pain to the basement workshop. Swaddled in an oversized shirt and shielded by safety goggles, I would eye the pattern on my drawing pad, consider the panes, select the perfect hue, and then grab a glass cutter. Compulsively.

Have you ever run a carbon blade across a sheet of glass and heard the silica sing? Then, applying pressure beneath the score line, seen a shower of slivers burst forth like so many mayflies? I have. Next comes the slow application of copper foil to the edges; the crimping and trimming; the reassembly of so many puzzle pieces; the application of acid; finally, the hot river of solder coursing along the copper path. You can lose yourself in the process. I did.

THAT SEASON I spent hundreds of dollars on copper foil, flux, solder, lead came, putty, and patina, but mostly on glass. Transparent and translucent. Rippled, hammered, seedy, Flemish, and Florentine. The sheets were tucked into a box custom-made to cradle them; twenty-odd years later, some rest there yet, including one piece, cerulean and snowy white.

The ghostly images didn't appear until I unwrapped my purchases at home, at least that's when I first noticed them. From the swirling, marbleized pattern emerged the profiles of two babies, side-by-side siblings, an unintentional death mask. I placed the pane in the box my husband built. It lies there still.

Are you a believer? Then maybe you would see angels in those opalescent silhouettes, think fate directed my hand to that sheet, imagine I was constructing a memorial window, and that pane was the centerpiece. I believe in the here and now, not the hereafter, in coincidence, and in the science of silica and metal oxides transformed in a fiery furnace.

But here we might agree: The healing arts have a twin in the healing crafts. Like glass, I was shattered; in the shard-by-shard reassembly we both became whole again.

My magnificent obsession eventually blanketed the house. Seeking daylight, the creations migrated from the basement to the first and second floors, every window a spectrum to behold. Friends and family acquired new views of the world, some insisting that I be paid for their pleasure. Expenses still far outweighed income. "Cheaper than therapy," I said.

Payback time arrived one fall weekend: a regional juried craft fair. The simple display my husband designed was packed into the car, two-by-four by two-by-four, along with my circles of color and light, and, expectantly, a cash box.

It was a long weekend at the county fairgrounds. I sold a single piece for $12.

No matter. By then I was pregnant, and hopeful.